Christian Martyrs for a Muslim People

Martin McGee, OSB

PAULIST PRESS
New York/Mahwah, NJ

Cover photograph by Karen Moller
Cover design by Joy Taylor
Book design by Lynn Else

Library of Congress Cataloging-in-Publication Data

McGee, Martin.
     Christian martyrs for a Muslim people / Martin McGee.
          p. cm.
     Includes bibliographical references.
     ISBN 978-0-8091-4539-3 (alk. paper)
     1. Christian martyrs—Algeria—Biography. 2. Catholic Church—Algeria—History—20th century. 3. Christianity and other religions—Islam. 4. Islam—Relations—Christianity. I. Title.
     BR1608.5.M39 2008
     272'.90965—dc22

                                                                        2008007525

Published by Paulist Press
997 Macarthur Boulevard
Mahwah, New Jersey 07430

www.paulistpress.com

Printed and bound in the
United States of America

Contents

CONTENTS

To Msgr. Henri Teissier
a Man of God
and
Lover of the Algerian People

Acknowledgments

I WOULD LIKE TO SAY a heartfelt thank you to all those who shared their insights and love of the Algerian Church and of Algeria with me, in particular Msgr. Henri Teissier; Sisters Janet Hotine, Lourdès Miguelez, and Marie-Pascale Nicolay; Fathers Thierry Becker, Henri Bonnamour, Armand Garin, Denis Gonalez, Pierre Lafitte, Jean-Marie Lassausse, John MacWilliam, and Jean-Belaïd Ould Aoudia.

I am very grateful to Msgr. Michael Fitzgerald for writing the foreword and to Jim Quigley at Paulist Press for his sensitive and helpful editing of the manuscript. I also would like to thank Alan Ogden, Sr. Mary Helen Jackson, and Sr. Janet Hotine for reading parts of this book and suggesting helpful changes. My thanks also go to Br. Anthony Brockman of Worth Abbey, who read the entire book and likewise made many valuable suggestions. Last but not least, I owe a great debt of gratitude to Abbot Christopher and my monastic brethren at Worth for supporting me in my interest in Algeria.

Some of the chapters have been previously published in *Religious Life Review* and *Spirituality,* two periodicals published by the Dominicans in Dublin. I am very grateful to their respective editors, Thomas McCarthy OP and Tom Jordan OP, for giving me permission to incorporate the following articles into this book:

"Pierre Claverie, OP, Witness to the Resurrection" (Chapter 10), *Religious Life Review* 41 (May/June2002).

"A Crucified Love" (reproduced in part in Chapter 9), *Religious Life Review* 42 (July/August 2003).

"The Gospel Life of Br. Henri Vergès" (Chapter 4), *Religious Life Review* 44 (May/June 2005).

"Any Common Ground between Christians and Islam" (reproduced in part in Chapter 11), *Spirituality* 9 (September/October 2003).

"Christian Martyrs for a Muslim People" (reproduced in part in Chapter 5), *Spirituality* 10 (November/December 2004).

"My Life Was Given to God and to This Country" (Chapter 8), *Spirituality* 12 (May/June 2006).

I am also grateful to the Association des Ecrits des Sept de l'Atlas, Abbaye Notre Dame d'Aiguebelle, 26230 Montjoyer, France, for granting me permission to use my own translation of Father Christian's *Testament* in Chapter 8.

Finally, I thank *La Semaine Religieuse d'Alger* for permission to reprint "To Offer One's Life Out of Love," and Msgr. Henri Teissier for permission to include his two unpublished addresses in English, "A Church Without Christians Which Is the Church of a Muslim People" and "Proclaiming the Gospel to Our Muslim Partners."

The Nineteen Algerian Martyrs, 1994–1996

Br. Henri Vergès, Marist Brother, born in Matemale, East Pyrenees, France, on July 15, 1930; assassinated in Algiers on May 8, 1994.

Sr. Paul-Hélène Saint-Raymond, Little Sister of the Assumption, born in Paris, France, on January 24, 1927; assassinated in Algiers on May 8, 1994.

Sr. Caridad Álvarez Martín, Augustinian Missionary Sister, born in Santa Cruz de la Salceda, Burgos, Spain, on May 9, 1933; assassinated in Algiers on October 23, 1994.

Sr. Esther Paniagua Alonso, Augustinian Missionary Sister, born in Izagre, Léon, Spain, on June 7, 1949; assassinated in Algiers on October 23, 1994.

Fr. Jean Chevillard, Missionary of Africa (White Father), born in Angers, France, on August 27, 1925; assassinated in Tizi-Ouzou, Algeria, on December 27, 1994.

Fr. Christian Chessel, Missionary of Africa (White Father), born in Digne, France, on October 27, 1958; assassinated in Tizi-Ouzou, Algeria, on December 27, 1994.

Fr. Charles Deckers, Missionary of Africa (White Father), born in Anvers, Belgium, on December 26, 1924; assassinated in Tizi-Ouzou, Algeria, on December 27, 1994.

Fr. Alain Dieulangard, Missionary of Africa (White Father), born in St-Brieuc, France, on May 21, 1919; assassinated in Tizi-Ouzou, Algeria, on December 27, 1994.

Sr. Bibiane Denise Leclercq, Sister of Our Lady of the Apostles, born in Gazerau, France, on January 8, 1930; assassinated in Algiers on September 3, 1995.

Sr. Angèle-Marie Jeanne Littlejohn, Sister of Our Lady of the Apostles, born in Tunis, Tunisia, on November 22, 1933; assassinated in Algiers on September 3, 1995.

Sr. Odette Prévost, Little Sister of the Sacred Heart, born in Oger, Champagne, France, on July 17, 1932; assassinated in Algiers on November 10, 1995.

Fr. Christian de Chergé, Cistercian monk (Trappist), born in Colmar, France, on January 18, 1937; assassinated near Médéa, Algeria, on May 21, 1996.

Br. Luc Dochier, Cistercian monk (Trappist), born in Bourg-de-Péage, France, on January 31, 1914; assassinated near Médéa, Algeria, on May 21, 1996.

Br. Paul Favre-Miville, Cistercian monk (Trappist), born in Vinzier, France, on April 17, 1939; assassinated near Médéa, Algeria, on May 21, 1996.

Br. Michel Fleury, Cistercian monk (Trappist), born in Sainte-Anne-sur-Brivet, France, on May 21, 1944; assassinated near Médéa, Algeria, on May 21, 1996.

Fr. Christophe Lebreton, Cistercian monk (Trappist), born in Blois, France, on October 11, 1950; assassinated near Médéa, Algeria, on May 21, 1996.

Fr. Célestin Ringeard, Cistercian monk (Trappist), born in Touvois, France, on July 29, 1933; assassinated near Médéa, Algeria, on May 21, 1996.

Fr. Bruno Lemarchand, Cistercian monk (Trappist), born in Saint-Maixent, France, on March 1, 1930; assassinated near Médéa, Algeria, on May 21, 1996.

Msgr. Pierre Claverie, Bishop of Oran, Algeria, Order of Preachers (Dominican), born in Algiers, Algeria, on May 8, 1938; assassinated in Oran, Algeria, on August 1, 1996.

Foreword

27 DECEMBER 1994

I was in Nouakchott, Mauritania, for the diocesan gathering held every year between Christmas and New Year. One evening I was invited to Eucharist and supper with the Sisters of Our Lady of Africa (White Sisters). Suddenly the news came that four of our brothers, Missionaries of Africa (White Fathers), had been assassinated in Tizi-Ouzou, Algeria. The tears flowed freely during the celebration, yet what could be a better way to try to understand this event than the reenactment of the sacrifice of Jesus? These four men had already given their lives through their commitment to Algeria and the Algerians. The violent death was only the consummation of this gift.

They were not the only ones to have lost their lives. The Catholic Church in Algeria counts nineteen religious as victims of the recent years of violence: six religious sisters, seven monks, one brother, four missionary priests, and one bishop. A number of other Christians, laypeople, also have been brutally murdered. Then there are the countless Algerian Muslims who have been eliminated too, perhaps as many as 200,000, the rotten fruit of a bloody conflict over what shape to give society in Algeria. The deaths of the nineteen have to be seen within this context.

Why do you stay in a place when you know you are in danger? Were these men and women seeking martyrdom? Were they of a superior breed of people, destined for glory? Were they better than their brothers and sisters, some of whom decided to return to their home countries, others who like them opted to stay in Algeria despite the threats to their lives? They stayed to show their solidarity with the Algerians among whom they were living and who had nowhere else to go. They stayed because they knew their presence was seen as a sign of hope, giving a glimpse of a different world where violence would not reign supreme. They stayed out of love.

They would surely not have considered themselves better than their fellow religious. Odette was killed, Chantal survived; yet they were both living the same vocation. Four Augustinian Sisters were walking to Mass and prudently decided to go in pairs. Esther and Caridad were the victims, but all four were motivated by the same dedication. Fortuitously Charlie Deckers was with his three confrères in Tizi-Ouzou on that 27 December; he did not belong to that particular community, but was only visiting. Pierre Claverie was one with his fellow bishops in Algeria; he was not their head, though often he acted as their spokesperson. The untimely end of each of these nineteen only brings out more clearly their devotedness, the logic of their dedicated lives, something that they shared with many others, with priests, religious, laypeople, men, and women. At the heart of these lives is Jesus, the Lord whom they chose to follow because he had chosen them, the Lord who had always loved his own in the world, but who now loved them to the end (John 13:1).

These nineteen lives given, because they were nineteen lives shared, bear a message that carries far beyond their country of adoption and death. They show how the Gospel can be preached in daily life. They show how a respectful dialogue or, perhaps better, a true encounter enables the Gospel to transcend boundaries. They show how the Church, in humble service and stripped of power, can be a sure sign of God's love, a sign indeed that God is Love. In the words of Pope Benedict XVI, "In a world where the name of God is sometimes associated with vengeance or even a duty of hatred and violence, this message is both timely and significant" (*Deus Caritas Est,* 1).[1]

> + *Michael L. Fitzgerald, M.Afr.*
> Apostolic Nuncio
> Egypt

Introduction

AS HAS BECOME OBVIOUS FROM happenings in recent years, the problems posed by Christian-Muslim relations have taken on a universal dimension. That is why the testimony of Fr. Martin McGee in this book makes a contribution that goes well beyond the specific problem posed by Christian-Muslim relations in Algeria. As part of his presentation of the martyrs of the Islamist crisis in Algeria, he proposes a stimulating reflection on what Christian-Muslim relations can become.

The context in which Fr. Martin's reflection is developed is in fact that of a particularly extreme period of violence and bloodshed between 1992 and 2000, a violence that is still active, even recently, although to a lesser extent. We know that for several years during the most serious period of the Algerian crisis, the United Kingdom was used as an operations base for the armed groups that caused so much blood to be shed in Algeria. At the exits of several London mosques money was collected to support these groups. Several of the bulletins of the GIA (Armed Islamic Group), which publicized their point of view, were in fact published in London by Muslims, British or otherwise, natives of the Middle East. They thus served as a link between Algeria and international public opinion.

However, what we have just recounted only evokes the negative side of these blood-soaked years. We must also discover the positive side. These years of crisis deepened the relationships between Christians and Muslims not only in Algeria itself, but also among numerous groups of people, Christian or Muslim, living in other countries and who were informed about what was going on, especially about the kidnapping and subsequent assassination of the seven monks. It is such a perspective that Fr. Martin brings to these events, and essentially that is why his work is a very valuable contribution to reflection on Christian-Muslim relations.

A Future That We Can Create Together

Msgr. Fitzgerald's foreword to this book proposes a very profound reflection on the martyrdom of nineteen of our brother priests and religious of the Algerian Church. I, for my part, would like to emphasize another aspect of Fr. Martin's work. Through the evocation of our victims, and in addition to their sacrifice, he makes known the relationships that exist at present in Algeria between Christians and many Algerian Muslims.

The very recent crisis in Palestine, in the Gaza Strip, and in Lebanon has shown once more to what extent peace will be endangered if the world today doesn't find a path that leads to dialogue with the peoples of Islam. We know the tensions that exist between Christians and Muslims, for example in northern Nigeria, in certain Indonesian islands, in the South of Sudan, and in many other countries where the two communities live together. We know how necessary it is for the future of peace to provide a positive solution to the current conflicts in Afghanistan, Iraq, Kashmir, and elsewhere.

But to draw attention to the places of tension between Christians and Muslims is not enough. We must also discover the places where Christians and Muslims acknowledge each other's common humanity, working together on the basis of their human or religious fraternity. In addition to the sacrifice of our victims, recounted in this text, Fr. Martin reveals the strength of the bonds which united these priests, these religious, to Muslim associates, and on a larger scale that of all of our Algerian Church to its Muslim environment.

In this sense the ecclesial experience lived out by the Algerian Christians can bring a message of hope for the future of Christian-Muslim collaboration. We experience here on a daily basis invaluable collaboration for the common good between Christians and Muslims. This collaboration creates trust and forms friendships. This is a new feature of Church witness. It has come about as a result of the openness of spirit created by Vatican II. It is a witness worth knowing because it speaks to us of a future that we can create together.

A Link Between Worth School and Algeria

The circumstances in which Fr. Martin came into contact with the Algerian Church are worth recalling. They can be seen as symbolic of the relations that current events are establishing between Great Britain and many Muslim countries. Everything started in the 1960s with the presence at Worth School—a well-known college attached to Worth Abbey of which Fr. Martin is currently chaplain—of a young British man, John MacWilliam, whose father was an officer in her Majesty's army living in the Gulf States. On leaving school the young John followed in his father's footsteps and became an officer who served successively in several Muslim countries of Africa and the Middle East.

Living in these countries, he was confronted daily with the reality and the compelling influence of the Muslim religion on society in the Arab world and also within a large number of African and Asian countries. The young officer, profoundly Christian, recognized his vocation to become a Catholic priest and missionary. Thereupon he decided to resign from the army and to enter the Missionaries of Africa (the White Fathers) who wish, as one of their primary objectives, to maintain a Christian presence in Muslim countries, especially on the African continent.

Having become a White Father and completed his training at the Pontifical Institute for Islamic & Arabic Studies in Rome, Fr. John was appointed to Tunisia in 1995. Following the assassination on December 27, 1994, of four of his fellow Missionaries of Africa, Fr. John volunteered to join the White Fathers in Algeria specifically to prepare the way, with a confrère, for a new community of White Fathers at Tizi-Ouzou. Algerian society was at that moment in a full-blown crisis, as has been already mentioned, with the increasing violence of the armed Islamic groups and the counter-violence of the security forces.

While awaiting an opportunity to reside permanently in Tizi-Ouzou, Fr. John helped out at the Diocesan Study Centre in Algiers, where he also set up a new lending library for Algerian Muslim students. Once at Tizi-Ouzou, he relaunched a project for the students, which had been started by the extinct community, by putting in place an English-language library for Algerian academics.

Fr. John, however, had never lost contact with Worth Abbey, in whose Church he had been ordained to the priesthood as a White Father in 1992. He goes back during his holidays not only out of loyalty to the school that had formed him, but also out of a desire to share his missionary commitment with the pupils of the school, where those in charge had, moreover, chosen to welcome some Muslim pupils. Following the announcement of the kidnapping of the seven monks from the monastery of Tibhirine, some of the pupils, made aware by their school of the international dimensions of Christian life, had decided to write to me, in my capacity as Archbishop of Algiers, to express their sympathy and their solidarity with me in this trial.

As the letter was in English and required a response in that language, I chose to entrust the reply to Fr. John, who was unaware of this initiative by his former school. Immediately upon reading this letter, and Fr. Martin's accompanying letter, he informed me that it came from an institution where he had been a pupil and with which he keeps strong links, especially with the monastic community. In this way a correspondence between Worth School and the Algerian Church was started. Fr. John encouraged me, should an opportunity present itself for me to go to England, to visit the school and to thus strengthen Fr. Martin's and his pupils' interest in Algeria.

A Visit to England

A little while later in 2002, the Anglican Church, supported by then prime minister Tony Blair, organized at Lambeth Palace an international seminar on Christian-Muslim relations. The British Ambassador presented me with an invitation in Algiers signed by the prime minister himself. I went to this gathering, whose conclusions have, moreover, been published.[1] It was also the occasion for my first visit to Worth Abbey and to Worth School. I was able to reply to the questions of the pupils responsible for the school magazine,[2] one of whom, a Muslim of Pakistani origin, was responsible for finishing the interview as his school friends had to leave to play in a match. I was also able to meet some parents, and I tried to explain to them the nature of Christian-Muslim encounter as we live it out in Algeria.

Encouraged by this visit, Fr. Martin began to get ready for his first trip to Algeria to discover on the spot the Christian-Muslim relations here. Impressed by several of the writings that our martyrs had authored before their deaths, he undertook to translate them for an English-speaking audience. About fifty books on the life of our Church during the Algerian crisis had already been published. But these writings were for the most part in French, with the exception of a few Spanish, Italian, and Arabic translations. Fr. Martin made his first visit from 7–14 April 2005. The following year he made another visit from 28 March to 8 April.

This contact with our ecclesial organization and with developments in Algeria, which was now emerging from the crisis, enabled him to write further articles about the witness of our Church during this period. Finally, it seemed to me that all these pieces deserved to be published, as English-speaking readers have no other means of becoming acquainted with the specific experience of our Church and its specific contribution to a more global reflection on Christian-Muslim relations. I asked Fr. Martin to revise these pieces and Msgr. Fitzgerald, who is well acquainted with our situation, to write a foreword. Msgr. Fitzgerald was until this year in charge of Christian-Muslim relations at the Vatican, and he is now fulfilling a similar role in his new post as Apostolic Nuncio to Egypt and the Arab League.

I commend this book to you.

+*Henri Teissier*
Archbishop of Algiers
July 2006

PART I:

The Background

CHAPTER ONE

A Fire Burning Inside

ON THURSDAY, APRIL 7, 2005, I looked out of the airplane window and saw the Algerian coastline for the first time. The plane landed without a hitch; the airport formalities went off equally smoothly and, feeling slightly anxious, I made my way into the arrivals hall and proceeded outside where the temperature was 29°C. What had brought a monk from Worth Abbey in Sussex to Houari Boumediene airport, Algiers, just as a brutal civil war was petering out? I had come at the invitation of Msgr. Henri Teissier, Archbishop of Algiers, to experience and savor a tiny Christian community, which between 1994 and 1996 had given the Church nineteen martyrs, nineteen lives freely offered out of love for their Muslim brothers and sisters. Their story had set a fire burning in my heart. And now I had come to meet their archbishop and live for one short week among a people for whom I felt a great empathy and a growing love.

A Growing Fascination with Algeria

The kidnapping of the seven monks of Tibhirine in March 1996 by the GIA, an Islamic armed group, had made media headlines throughout the world. Strangely enough I can't recall following the story. The English newspapers would not have found it highly newsworthy as all of the monks were either of French or of *pied-*

noir extraction.[1] In fact, the plight of the Christian remnant in Algeria only gradually gripped my imagination, and the person responsible for this was Msgr. Henri Teissier, Archbishop of Algiers. On January 12, 1997, The Tablet featured an interview with Msgr. Teissier that deeply impressed me. I sensed something of his love for the Algerian people and his conviction that the Gospel was truly Good News, something of ultimate importance. The journalist wrote that he "was moved by [his] visit to a priest of such dedication and fortitude." His courage and desire to stay alongside the Algerian people in their hour of need touched me.

I then forgot about the article and got on with the busy-ness of school mastering and living the monastic round. A few months later I referred to Msgr. Teissier's courageous witness in a homily at mass. I compared his willingness to risk his life for his flock to Jesus' sacrificial act of love for us in the Eucharist. Shortly afterward, I suddenly felt that I should write to Archbishop Teissier to offer a word of support. I didn't have his address and just sent my short letter to the *Archevêque d'Alger, Alger, Algeria* and promptly forgot all about it. To my surprise, a few months later a reply arrived, written on behalf of the Archbishop by Fr. John MacWilliam, a former student of Worth School. I didn't know that Fr. John was in Algeria so this added another twist to the plot.

A First Visit to Algeria

Discovering this unknown link with Algeria whetted my interest. Fr. John MacWilliam came to visit Worth School and monastery on a few occasions and so my interest grew. I hadn't considered the possibility of visiting Algeria because of the high level of violence at this time. In 2003, I became aware that the violence had decreased dramatically, and a trip, or rather a pilgrimage, to Algeria might be possible. In the summer of 2004, I visited the Tibhirine community that had regrouped in Morocco after the beheading of seven members of the community south of Algiers in 1996. Worries about traveling on my own to the unknown world of North Africa were lessening and, encouraged by some of my monastic brethren, I decided that it was now or never. So I emailed two people in Algiers, putting out feelers as to the possibility of traveling there. The first request received no reply. The second, sent a few weeks later, also drew a blank. The silence was ominous. Having asked the intercession of several of the saints and of Notre-Dame D'Afrique, there was still deep silence. I decided that I would have to give up this dream as it wasn't meant to be. The Lord wasn't in it. I put the Algerian pilgrimage out of my mind and, to keep in contact with things French, I set about arranging a week's stay with a religious community in France. Just as I was about to buy the air ticket I received an email from Msgr. Teissier inviting me to come and stay with him at the Diocesan House: "We will welcome you with great joy." The second person whom I had emailed had forwarded my letter to the Archbishop. So my prayers had been answered, but only after I had first accepted an apparent no.

In the airport lounge I felt suddenly quite anxious, almost as if I were taking my life in my hands. I had read a lot about the pervasive violence and now it all felt very real. However, this minor attack of anxiety quickly faded as I didn't sense any air of menace inside or outside the airport. The atmosphere felt a little subdued but nothing worse. On my arrival at the Diocesan House I was surprised to find the courtyard bustling with a group of visiting French priests who were about to set off for the airport. In the confusion Msgr. Teissier said goodbye to me, mistaking me for one of the departing priests! A few minutes later when calm had returned I introduced myself to the Archbishop. We had met once before when he had briefly visited Worth in January 2002. He greeted me warmly and we then proceeded up to his apartment for a drink. Msgr. Teissier, an energetic man with a great sense of humor, told me told me that I would be addressing that evening a group of twenty-six Muslim students who were staying for the weekend in the Diocesan House. I knew then that my visit wasn't going to be a dull affair.

A Meeting with Muslim Students

The twenty-six students were training to run a holiday camp for youngsters who had been traumatized by the 2003 earthquake. So this was going to be my first encounter with this people for whom I felt a great attraction and affection without ever having met any of them before. How could that be, you may well ask. I am not sure that a clear answer can be given. The love-hate relationship of the French people with Algeria had drawn me, as a Francophile, to that country, as had the evocative novels and autobiography of Albert Camus, who was brought up in Algiers. The love of the nineteen martyrs for Algeria had also, undoubtedly, affected me deeply. They had been willing to sacrifice their lives out of love for this people and I had somehow sensed how worthy of being loved they were. Msgr. Teissier's willingness to give his life for them had also deeply impressed me. In a sense I was on a pilgrimage to discover the source of this love, which ultimately flows from Jesus' love for us, a love that impelled him to freely offer his life on our behalf. So perhaps here was to be found the deepest motivation for my strange interest and journey. Like the prophet Jeremiah I had a fire burning in my heart, a fire that refused to go out.

On meeting the Muslim students, what most struck me was how much at home they were in the Diocesan House; they were every bit at home there as a group of Catholic students would be at Worth. There was a very friendly and relaxed atmosphere. I was unsure as to what I would have to say. So, apart from explaining how I had ended up in Algeria, I used my teaching skills to dialogue a little with them. Msgr. Teissier chipped in now and again with a clarification. There was one awkward question when a student asked what I knew about Algeria. I had to admit that in fact I knew very little about the country. After about forty minutes the students entertained us with some sketches. I found them highly amusing as they were poking fun at the idiocies of bureaucracy, an experience to which most of us can quite easily relate. I said good-night to the students, having thoroughly enjoyed myself and having had experienced a strong sense of rapport with them. I had even enjoyed greatly their sense of humor. Yes, this visit had got off to a blessed start.

Remembering the Martyrs of Tizi-Ouzou

On Sunday afternoon I set off for Tizi-Ouzou with Msgr. Teissier, Br. Johannes Heuft, and a visiting Belgian priest. At Tizi-Ouzou four White Fathers had been assassinated on December 27, 1995, a few hours after the young superior, Christian Chessel, had been given the all clear by the local authorities to construct a new library for use by the nearby university students. The White Fathers had taken up residence once more and the new library was nearing completion. On arrival I was shown the temporary library where a few students were present. The high point of our visit was the celebration of mass with a small congregation of about a dozen local Christians. Normally there would have been a much larger congregation during university term time, thanks to the presence of African students. Msgr. Teissier introduced the mass recalling that it was here in this location that four White Fathers had given their lives out of love for the people. This was a moving moment as Msgr. Teissier's few simple words poignantly evoked the laying down of their lives for us. The mass was made more special by the presence of three young Berber Christians, two of whom had recently joined the Christian community.

The Emptiness of Tibhirine

When I arrived in Algiers I told Msgr. Teissier that there were two things above all which I would like to do: firstly, to visit the Basilique Notre-Dame d'Afrique, which has witnessed so many key moments in the life of the Algerian Church and, secondly, to visit Tibhirine, the monastery of the assassinated Trappist monks. Msgr. Teissier, attentive to my wishes, arranged for Fr. Jean-Marie Lassausse to pick me up from the Diocesan House at 7:00 a.m. on Monday so that I could join him at Tibhirine for the day. Fr. Jean-Marie was now in charge of the monastery buildings and land as the Archbishop had failed, despite valiant efforts, to find a new community to take up residence at Tibhirine. The remaining two monks of Tibhirine, Jean-Pierre and Amédée, had transferred Notre-Dame de l'Atlas, first to Fès in Morocco on June 2, 1996, and then, in 2000, to Midelt in the center of the same country. An effort had been made by the Trappists to maintain a presence in the Nunciature in Algiers, where the community of Notre-Dame de Tibhirine, under the leadership of Fr. Jean-Claude, a former bursar of Cîteaux, was established. When it became clear that there was no immediate prospect of returning to Tibhirine on account of the continuing violence, a decision was taken to dissolve the community. Tibhirine is now cared for by the Archdiocese of Algiers and Jean-Marie spends three days a week there looking after the grounds and buildings with the help of two full-time employees, both villagers. The guest house has been renovated and some groups and individuals are now able to spend time there on retreat. The security situation, though much improved, still gives cause for concern, so finding a new religious community to live at Tibhirine will not be easy.

I had been a little apprehensive about the trip to Tibhirine. On the previous Thursday, April 7, fourteen people had been assassinated by three armed Islamic terrorists at a *faux-barrage,* a fake roadblock, on the road to Tablat, not far from Médéa. The final toll of fourteen dead included two children from the same family aged five and ten. Five vehicles and eleven of the victims were burned to a cinder and two died of bullet wounds. The ambush occurred at 7:20 p.m. All the victims were civilians.[2]

Such events have been, of course, commonplace in the country since the start of the civil war in 1992, though their frequency has greatly decreased in recent years. My slight unease about safety was in fact groundless, as these ambushes occur after dark and tend to be on minor roads. Jean-Pierre had agreed with the police that for safety reasons he would leave Tibhirine before nightfall. In addition, the police and army presence on the road to Médéa was dense. A small watchtower stood every mile or so along the road, and there were numerous police and army checkpoints. The road for the final seven kilometers of the journey from Médéa to Tibhirine was badly potholed, and the sludge and cold created an impression of hardship and austerity.

All the pictures that I had seen of the monastery had failed to give me a feeling for either it or its surroundings. Tibhirine is at an altitude of 1100 meters and there were still patches of snow on the ground. It looks east toward the mountains, and the rugged scenery was gradually becoming more colorful with the approach of spring. The monastery hadn't been occupied for more than nine years, and the buildings, dilapidated and austere, were without heating and decidedly cold inside.

My second impression was that of absence. I was conscious of emptiness at the heart of Tibhirine. Even the presence of the cemetery with the carefully tended graves of the seven martyrs failed to make a difference. There was certainly peacefulness there but also an undeniable sense of absence. The Abbot General of the Order, Dom Olivera, wrote of his strong feelings on the day of the monks' burial at Tibhirine, "A single phrase was resounding in my heart, 'We will not leave our dead alone, we shall come back!' We left at 2:00 p.m.—without leaving."[3] As long as the Trappist monks are left alone in the graveyard I fear that the atmosphere at Tibhirine will continue to be one of emptiness.

A Remarkable Church

And so my week progressed as I visited the places associated with the martyrs and the various libraries and other institutions run by the Church. Everywhere I sensed a spirit of energy, friendship, and optimism. I came to understand and to appreciate more and more the riches of a Church that had produced nineteen martyrs. In this book I will try to share with you something of the life of this remarkable Church and the story of her martyrs. To understand fully the story of the martyrs, we need to know something about the social and theological context of the tiny Church that nurtured them. These martyrs of charity did not stumble unknowingly into death but offered their lives freely out of love for a Muslim people. To understand the motivation for their courageous decision to stay on in Algeria and to face death daily, we need to know something of the Church that produced them and of her theology of Christian-Muslim encounter. It is this Church and her theological understanding of her raison d'être in an overwhelmingly Muslim country that gives us the key to their witness. This is a story that we in the West would do well to listen to as we seek to integrate a growing Muslim presence into a traditionally Christian culture, a story which, I hope, will give us a deeper understanding of Christian-Muslim encounter.

CHAPTER TWO

Confronted by Death

A Church and Society in Turmoil

THE DECLINE AND ALMOST TOTAL disappearance of the Christian Church in Algeria in the second half of the twentieth century is not something new, nor is the phenomenon of martyrdom.[1] The martyred Cyprian of Carthage was a bishop of the North African Church. Her most famous son is the great Doctor of the Church, Saint Augustine, who had his Episcopal seat at Hippo, now called Annaba, in Algeria. In the fifth century the borders of modern day Algeria contained as many as 296 bishoprics. Weakened by the Donatist crisis and the Vandal invasion, the Christian Church was more or less completely wiped out by the Arab-Muslim invasion between the seventh and the twelfth centuries. What we know as Algeria today has experienced seven large-scale invasions and colonizations: the Phoenicians–Carthaginians, 1100–146 BC; the Romans, 146 BC–AD 432; the Vandals, 432–533; the Byzantines, 533–633; the Arabs, 755–1516; the Turks, 1516–1830; and finally the French, 1830–1962.[2] Between the twelfth and the nineteenth centuries there was a very small Christian presence made up of captives, diplomats, mercenaries, traders, and members of religious orders such as the Franciscans, Dominicans, and the Vincentians. The latter first set foot in Algeria in 1646–1648 and are still present today. One of their members, Jordi Llambrich, was ordained priest in Algiers on June 24, 2005, by Msgr. Teissier, the first priestly ordination in Algeria since that of Fr. Christophe of Tibhirine in January 1990.

THE WHITE FATHERS

With the landing of the French forces at Sidi-Ferruch in 1830 a new era in the life of the Church began, namely that of a colonial presence made up of European settlers from France, Spain, Italy, and Malta. Although there was no integration between the colonials and the indigenous Muslim population, efforts were made by Cardinal Lavigerie and the order which he founded, The Missionaries of Africa (better known as The White Fathers), to understand and respect the native religion and culture. This respect for the native religion and culture was also encouraged by Charles de Foucauld and the many spiritual congregations inspired by his life and teaching which were to spring up after his death in 1916, such as The Little Brothers and The Little Sisters of Jesus. The White Fathers still play a vital role in the life of the Christian Church in Algeria, and four of its members were numbered among the nineteen martyrs of the 1990s.

The White Fathers were founded by Cardinal Lavigerie in 1868 to spread Christianity among the Muslims of North Africa and the "pagans" of the sub-Sahara. Msgr. Lavigerie was conscious of the enormity of the challenge that he had set his missionary society. He fully realized that Christianity would take a long time to take root in African soil, particularly in Islamic countries. He wasn't interested in instant conversions, conversions that had no prospect of enduring in a hostile environment. To be baptized, a candidate had to undergo a four-year catechumenate or training period, and this rule applied to children as well as to adults. In addition, children could only be baptized with the written consent of both parents.[3]

As well as the witness of prayer and community life, the missionaries were to establish contact with the local population through humanitarian works: medical assistance, agricultural education, and schools. These works were a concrete expression of the great Christian virtue of love of neighbor, "charity towards the inhabitants, not just by way of winning their sympathy, but simply because we and they are sons of the self-same God."[4] Importantly, the missionaries were to take on the lifestyle of the people and not seek to turn them into Europeans: "Rather, make yourselves what they are, as far as your priesthood permits. Speak their language, adopt their customs, live among them as the brothers to them that you are. Even should they become Christians, encourage them to retain all of their culture which does not conflict outright with their new faith."[5] The four martyrs of Tizi-Ouzou, each in his own way, exemplified the spirit of inculturation and respect for the Muslim faith that Lavigerie advocated in those far-off days when terms such as *ecumenism* and *interfaith dialogue* had not yet been coined. However, not withstanding this cultural sensitivity of the missionaries, the Church presence under French rule was essentially focused on providing for the needs of the European Christian settlers.

THE DEATH OF A CHURCH

The plight of the tiny Christian community in Algeria came to the attention of the English-speaking world with the assassination of the seven Cistercian monks of Tibhirine in 1996 and of Pierre Claverie, OP, the bishop of Oran, shortly afterward. Since 1992, when the first round of the general election was cancelled for fear of an Islamic Salvation Front victory, Islamic fundamentalists and a military-dominated government have been involved in a violent and ruthless civil war. An estimated one hundred thousand to two hundred thousand people have lost their lives in the merciless killing of men, women, and children. And the tiny Christian community has also borne its share of the violence. In 1993 all foreigners in Algeria were ordered by the GIA (Armed Islamic Group) to leave the country or die. Between 1994 and 1996 about one hundred Christians lost their lives and nineteen priests and religious, eighteen in the Archdiocese of Algiers, were assassinated as they went about their daily work of serving the poorest sections of Algerian society. The Catholic community in the four dioceses in Algeria has now been reduced to a shadow of its former self, numbering perhaps as few as three thousand members.

With Algerian independence in 1962 the Christian Church was to undergo what Archbishop Teissier describes as "three stages in the death of a Church."[6] The first followed directly after independence when, over a period of a few months, nine hundred thousand European settlers departed. With them went nearly all of the few thousand native Christians of Algerian and Muslim origin. In the years following independence, about seven hundred churches or chapels were handed over by the Church to be turned into mosques. However, the arrival of volunteer workers, *les coopérants,* as technical assistants to the new Algerian state brought new life to the Christian community. A further blow to morale occurred, however, in 1976 when all the Church's schools, hospitals, and other social services were taken over by the government as part of a general nationalization program.

The second stage in the death of the Church took place in 1993 when all foreigners were ordered out of the country under threat of death by the GIA. The subsequent assassinations of foreign workers and the closure of all the foreign schools—French, American, Italian, German, Russian, Polish—meant that almost all the Christian families left the country, as did many of the European spouses of Algerians who also feared for their lives. With the collapse of the local currency, the dinar, the Coptic coopérants (Christian aid workers) from Egypt also left. The few thousand native Algerian Christians had begun to leave the country after independence and this new outbreak of violence accelerated the departure of those who had remained.

The third stage in the death of the Church occurred with the assassination of the nineteen religious and priests between

1994 and 1996. A good indication of the collapse of the Christian presence in Algeria can be seen in the statistics of the Archdiocese of Algiers. In 1970, eight years after independence, there were an estimated fifty thousand Catholics (1.1 percent of the total population of just under 4 1/2 million) looked after by eighty-nine diocesan priests and ninety-three priests belonging to religious orders. By 1988 the number of Catholics had fallen to twenty-eight thousand with a total of ninety-seven priests. Of the 222 religious sisters in the archdiocese of Algiers in 1993, there remained three years later a total of seventy. By 1999, in the wake of Islamist violence, the number of Catholics had fallen to 1,250 and the number of priests to forty-seven.[7] The remaining few thousand Christians in the country as a whole are made up of elderly Europeans who remained on after independence, spouses of mixed marriages, workers on the Saharan oil refineries, about a thousand African students on scholarships at Algerian universities, diplomats, and the few remaining Algerian Christians. Today all that remains of a once thriving Christian community in Algeria is about three thousand Christians and three hundred religious and priests in a country of thirty-three million people.[8]

A MORE EVANGELICAL WITNESS

These crises for the Church, however painful they may have been, however they may have stripped the Church of her power and prestige, have nevertheless resulted in a more evangelical witness. As a result of the traumas of the war of independence and the recent civil war, the Church has found a new identity in Algeria. The Church now lives alongside the Algerian people and shares in its sufferings and joys. The departure of the European population and the 1976 nationalization of the remaining Church institutions, especially its schools, freed the religious orders to concentrate on the needier sections of the local Muslim population: running literacy courses in parishes, opening educational projects for women, establishing libraries for students, administering retirement communities, providing support services for those with disabilities, offering preemployment courses, and even teaching Arabic. The remaining Christians in the Catholic tradition do not see their presence in terms of maintaining a chaplaincy role for resident foreigners. As Msgr. Teissier puts it: "Thus gradually we all grew in the conviction that the Algerian Church was the Church of Algeria, that is to say a reality in a relationship with a Muslim society and finding its *raison d'être* in this relationship. The Church wasn't an end in itself as would be the case of a Chaplaincy serving only its own members. But Christians were united in a specific vocation of establishing an evangelical relationship with a Muslim people."[9]

In the light of the teaching of Vatican II, Christians were led to recognize more clearly the Spirit at work both in the spiritual tradition of Islam and in efforts by people of goodwill to promote the dignity of the human person. It was in this context, as we shall see later, that the understanding of the Church as a "Church of Encounter" has been developed. This is a theology that sees God's Spirit at work in both traditions, Christian and Muslim, and that is open to the gifts that each side has to offer the other.

The Political Crisis

From 1962, the date of independence, until 1988 Algeria was a single-party socialist state. This party, the FLN (National Liberation Front), was made up of a coalition of army chiefs, a few political personalities who had gained their legitimacy through being associated with the war of liberation, technical advisers, and FLN executives who supposedly represented the people. A program of nationalization and industrialization funded by oil revenues was quickly implemented, as was a program of arabization of the education system and the civil service. One unfortunate result of the arabization program was the recruitment of educators from

Qur'anic schools and other traditional establishments. Those recruited from abroad, in particular the Egyptians, often propagated a fundamentalist understanding of the Islamic tradition. A weakness inherent to the situation was the lack of properly trained religious leaders in Algeria. Until President Chadli succeeded Boumediene in 1978, there were no third-level training institutions available for religious leaders in Algeria. As a result, there were very few people equipped to counter the fundamentalist interpretations of the Qur'an being propagated by Ali Belhadj and other extremists. These Islamists claimed that they were authorized by God to purify both Muslim societies and the world of all infidels.

THE END OF ONE PARTY RULE

With oil prices dropping from $30 to $10 dollars per barrel in 1985–86, the FLN socialist program ran out of steam—there was a shortage of consumer goods and of certain foodstuffs, and the young had neither jobs nor proper housing. The ensuing frustration, especially of the jobless young who had come to the conclusion that the government was corrupt and uncaring, led to a popular uprising in October 1988. In this uprising on the streets of Algiers and of other cities, 159 people were killed. As a result, the State was forced to give up one-party rule. Between 1989 and 1992 other political parties were recognized, the press was given more freedom, and voluntary associations and the market economy were encouraged. Many people concluded that the corruption brought about by a single-party state could only be overcome by a return to religion and the social justice that it promised. In this context of popular discontent, the Islamic movement gained strength and the FIS, Islamic Salvation Front, took 188 out of 430 seats in the first round of the legislative elections in December 1991. And they were poised to take 144 more seats in the second round to give them a crushing majority, the FLN having gained only fifteen seats in the first round.

SUPPRESSION OF THE FIS

The army, frightened by the prospect of an Islamist government that would take away its power, cancelled the second round of elections scheduled for January 16, 1992, and forced the president to resign. They recalled Mohamed Boudiaf, a founding member of the FLN and hero of the fight for independence, from exile in Morocco to install him as president of the High Council of State. Large numbers of the FIS militants were arrested—estimates range from five thousand by the army to thirty thousand by the FIS—and the party was officially suppressed by the government on March 4. This suppression of the electoral process led in its turn to an armed rebellion by the Islamists, which still runs its course today. Since then democratic elections have been reinstated with the election of President Zeroual in June 1995, followed by the election of a legislative assembly in June 1997 and municipal elections in October 1997. In December 1997 a second chamber, the Council of the Nation, was inaugurated, and finally the High Islamic Council was established in January 1998.

THE ARMED ISLAMIC OPPOSITION

The armed Islamic opposition gradually divided into two groups, the AIS, Islamic Army of Salvation, affiliated to the FIS, and the more radical GIA, Armed Islamic Group. The AIS declared a unilateral cease-fire on October 1, 1997, and responded to the offer of an amnesty by President Bouteflika in 1999. The more radical GIA refuses all negotiation with the State. It is made up of various armed groupings under leaders known as *emirs*. The GIA quickly began to target not only the police and military but also intellectuals, journalists, imams, foreigners, and artists. As the cities became more secure, attacks were directed at the poor in isolated villages and unprotected suburbs. The civilian population became the victims of fake roadblocks, car bombs, massacres, and other atrocities. In 1997 and 1998, the GIA guerrillas started massacring entire villages and neighborhoods, killing on some occasions hundreds of innocent civilians regardless of age or sex. Anyone not supporting the GIA was considered to be an apostate and hence subject to the death penalty. "The areas south and east of Algiers, which had voted strongly for FIS in 1991, were hit particularly hard; the Rais and Bentalha massacres in particular shocked worldwide observers. Pregnant women were sliced open, children were hacked to pieces or dashed against walls, men's limbs were hacked off one by one, and, as the attackers retreated, they would kidnap young women to keep as sex slaves."[10] The population, growing tired of the indiscriminate violence of the GIA, withdrew its support. The Salafist Group for Preaching and Combat (GSPC) is now the most active terrorist movement in Algeria, with an estimated four hundred to six hundred guerrilla fighters mainly in the center of the country. This group broke away from the GIA in 1996. Although it has the same aim of setting up an Islamic state, unlike the GIA, it focuses its attacks on the army and security forces and claims that it tries to avoid inflicting civilian causalities. The number of active Islamic guerrilla fighters is thought to be approximately eight hundred to one thousand, down from a high of 25,000 at the height of the civil war in the mid-1990s. In January 2007, the GSPC changed its name to The Al-Qaeda Organization in the Islamic Maghreb.

A 1988 report commissioned by the Secretary General of the United Nations stated: "In recent years Algeria has seen significant changes. It now has an elected president, an elected parliament in which ten political parties are represented and a second chamber, the Council of the Nation. There is lively debate in parliament. There is also ostensible separation of the executive branch from the military and judiciary branches. Nevertheless, some Algerians think that the military still plays an important role in the conduct of the country's affairs and still has a crucial influence."[11] With the resignation of President Zeroual a new president,

Abdelaziz Bouteflika, was elected with 74 percent of the votes on April 15, 1999, and reelected in 2004 with 83.49 percent of the votes. Bouteflika offered an amnesty to all Islamist guerrillas who had not taken part in massacres, rape, or the bombing of public places. This amnesty was approved by referendum on September 16, 1999, and a good number of guerrillas took the opportunity to repent and return to civilian life. A second amnesty was also overwhelmingly approved by the people in September 2005. At present the GIA appear to have ceased operating and most guerrilla attacks are now claimed by the GSPC. The number of deaths as a result of guerrilla attacks has fallen greatly and most parts of the country now enjoy peace. At present the number of Islamist guerrillas in the country is probably at most one thousand.

The Future Challenge

A great challenge faces the country in the economic and social fields. Not only must Algeria cope with the transition to a market-led economy, but it must also deal with the consequences of the economic destruction wrought by years of terrorism. However, an even greater challenge is posed by the moral disarray of the people. This has been a result of the corruption associated with the years of single-party rule, the faltering arrival of democracy, and in particular the use of religion to justify the indiscriminate killing of the innocent. It is in this context of moral drift and uncertainty that the story of the martyrs and the witness of the tiny Christian remnant have such a powerful role to play.

CHAPTER THREE

Cardinal Duval

The Power of Friendship

CARDINAL DUVAL COULD BE CALLED the founding father of the Catholic Church in post-colonial Algeria. One of the keys to understanding the life and witness of the martyrs and the continuing witness of the tiny Christian community in Algeria can be found in the story of his friendship with the Algerian people and with Islam.

Ascetic in appearance, reserved in temperament, and unable to speak Arabic, Léon-Étienne Duval was at first sight an unlikely person to hold this pivotal position. Appointed Archbishop of Algiers in 1954, it fell to him to guide the Church during the war of independence, 1954–1962, and in its aftermath when Church membership was decimated by the departure of most of the European settlers. Above all, he was faced with the daunting task of reconciling Christian and Muslim, a task still at the forefront in Algeria today and in other parts of the world.

Léon-Étienne Duval was born in the Haute-Savoie in France on December 9, 1903, the sixth of seven children. His family was profoundly Catholic, and many of his relations were priests or religious, including three of his sisters. His parents owned a medium-sized farm and Léon was spared some of the harder work as his health was delicate. After the junior seminary, he continued his priestly formation at the French Seminary in Rome and attended the Jesuit-run Gregorian University, where he discovered

21

the writings of the Algerian, Saint Augustine, who was to become a lifelong companion. The death of his elder brother in the First World War, when Léon was just eleven years old, marked him deeply and confirmed his desire to become a priest. Msgr. Duval later commented, "Suffering, I have encountered it in every year of my existence since my childhood."[1] Ordained a priest in 1926, he was appointed professor of philosophy and dogmatic theology in the diocesan seminary at Annecy from 1930 to 1938, and in 1942 he became vicar general of the diocese. The Second World War brought him into contact with many social and moral issues including that of resistance to the Nazis. War and violence were to be his constant companions throughout life.

Bishop of Constantine

In November 1946, Msgr. Duval was nominated bishop of Constantine and Hippo in Algeria by Pius XII, Hippo having been the diocese of the great Saint Augustine. Ordained Bishop on February 11, 1947, in Annecy, he set foot in Algeria for the first time on February 23. On landing at Algiers, he was met by the Archbishop, Msgr. Leynaud, and by his childhood friend, Msgr. Jacquier, who was now vicar general of the archdiocese of Algiers. Even before his arrival in Algeria, Msgr. Duval sensed that colonization had had its day. From the beginning he was struck by the problems that faced his adopted country. As he traveled by train from Algiers to Constantine to take up his Episcopal charge he remarked: "At each station where the train stopped—except in the towns—I saw groups of miserably dressed children holding out their hands and, in a pleading voice, asking for alms, a sign of a grave social disorder."[2] He found the extent of the social problems and their inevitable consequences frightening. Poverty also affected sections of the European population. Once while walking near the town of Skikda to his great horror he saw "a European woman who was living in a cave: the entry was covered by a floor cloth. I was ashamed of being correctly dressed and I didn't dare enter…There is an abyss between the knowledge which one can obtain of poverty in books or newspapers and the encounter with the reality of poverty in the lives of people."[3]

In the midst of this tense period leading up to the collapse of the colonial régime in 1962, Msgr. Duval always drew inspiration and solace from the teachings of Saint Augustine. He found them inspiring, especially in relation to his pastoral role as bishop, which involved a concern for the well-being of both the Catholic and Muslim population. For Saint Augustine, love of God and love of neighbor were inseparable. One of Msgr. Duval's favorite quotations from Saint Augustine was "brotherly love is the first and the last step in attaining the love of God."[4] This eminently practical teaching of Augustine encouraged Cardinal Duval in his preaching of more just and loving relationships between the European colonizers and the Muslim majority. However, for him the indispensable companion of justice, its soul if you like, was love: "Justice is necessary to get rid of the causes of poverty in the structures of society. But fraternal love gives justice its vigor and its creative strength. Without love, people lack the imagination to implement justice."[5] Already as Bishop of Constantine, Msgr. Duval hadn't equated the European presence with the presence of Christianity nor did he see a future for colonialism.

Fidelity to the Gospel Message

In February 1954, Msgr. Duval was appointed Archbishop of Algiers, succeeding Msgr. Leynaud who had held office for over a third of a century. He had just a few months in which to settle into his new post before the start of the war of independence on November 1. No one, least of all the military commanders, was expecting such an event. He was convinced that a long-term solution to the political aspirations of the Algerian people must be founded on justice for all. This would involve friendship with the Muslim population based on respect and equality. He states, "I often alerted the conscience of Catholics to the injustices which the situation in Algeria concealed."[6] His warnings, unfortunately, were not heeded and the traumatic war of independence was unleashed on settlers and natives alike.

Cardinal Duval was a man of clear Christian principles. He had the ability to enunciate moral principles in a way that could be understood by both Christian and Muslim alike. Msgr. Duval taught that the Christian faith was not tied to any political party or country, but that its teachings were based on fraternal love and friendship and had as their aim the defense of the dignity of the human person. It demanded great moral courage to clearly state the Gospel message without any partisanship in a war that pitted the one million Christian Europeans against nine million native Muslims. Msgr. Duval reiterated time and time again the basic Christian position on torture and violence—what was at stake was the honor of God, which was betrayed when human beings were abused; evil means could not be justified to obtain a good end. Rather the solution lay in living out the Christian message of fraternal service and love which alone would lead to a lasting and peaceful cohabitation for the three major faiths in Algeria (before independence, there was also a sizeable Jewish community). In all of his teaching, Cardinal Duval was careful to support his points with quotations from relevant Vatican documents. However, what strikes the reader, even today, is the simplicity and evangelical tone of his statements. Above everything else he wished to be faithful to the Gospel message. In a statement on May 30, 1954, a few months before the outbreak of war, we see Msgr. Duval's very concrete and unambiguous application of the Gospel: "We must not forget that in the eyes of God there are no privileged classes, no privileged races or families; there are no privileged professions. All persons have a right to life and to all that is necessary for life. The great law among peoples is that of universal brotherhood."[7]

On January 17, 1955, two-and-a-half months after the start of war, he issued his first condemnation of torture by the government forces. And on October 7, 1956, he wrote about "the necessity to accede gradually to the request of the Algerian people for self-determination,"[8] three years before General de Gaulle came to the same conclusion. However, Cardinal Duval was not seeking to play a political party role; in fact, he saw the confusion of party politics and Christianity as a great danger. All of his many interventions and declarations were made as the guardian of the Christian conscience. Msgr. Duval was unceasing in his efforts to defend the dignity of the human person without making distinctions between Algerian and European: "To offend gravely a human person is to insult God's majesty...torture continues to be practiced; villages are destroyed, summary executions take place; people disappear without anyone knowing what has become of them. The youth of France runs the risk of being corrupted when it is made to take part in actions contrary to morality."[9]

A Costly Witness to Friendship

This speaking out of an unpopular Gospel to the *pieds-noirs*, or European settlers, was made at a huge personal cost. He was derided as Mohammed Duval in the press and on several occasions his churches were bombed by the OAS (Organisation de l'armée secrète—an armed group founded in 1961 to oppose the granting of Algerian independence). The Cardinal, however, was blessed with great courage strengthened by his evangelical convictions and understanding of his responsibilities as a bishop. His main fear was not of offending people but rather of offending God: "I have always lived in the fear of God and in fear of failing to live up to my charge as bishop."[10] Msgr. Duval knew from the depth of his own suffering how costly being faithful to the Gospel could be. He noted that each year of his life had been marked by suffering. Undoubtedly, one of the blackest of years was 1976, when his dear childhood friend and auxiliary bishop, Msgr. Jacquier, was stabbed to death in the streets of Algiers by a mentally disturbed man. Suffering was to accompany him right to the end of his life.

Perhaps the whole of Cardinal Duval's ministry in Algeria could be summed up in the word *friendship* and its corollary *dialogue,* both of which he saw as the keys to the future. For him dialogue wasn't an abstract theological task but a question of the heart, of a relationship of love between individual Christians and Muslims. The Vatican II documents gave an official theological underpinning to this encounter between Christians and those of other faiths. However, even before the Council, the Cardinal was preaching and practicing what we now call interfaith or interreligious dialogue. In his radio broadcast for Pentecost 1956, he stated that the Holy Spirit "is sent even outside the visible Church to all people of goodwill."[11] He points out that in dialogue with people of other faiths, or of none, God may be speaking through them to remind us of Gospel truths.

The Revolutionary Power of Brotherly Love

In his Pastoral Letter for Lent, 1980, *Présence Fraternelle,*[12] Msgr. Duval outlined succinctly the three levels at which dialogue may take place. First of all there is a "dialogue of the heart," that is to say, the development of friendships between Christians and Muslims. Secondly, there is a "dialogue of life," which involves working together for the promotion of human values having their foundation in faith in God. And finally there is dialogue at the doctrinal level, where participants seek to understand each other's Church teaching in a clear and unprejudiced manner. However, "Nothing is possible without real friendship."[13] And of course friendship assumes mutual respect and an acknowledgment of God's presence in each other. The Cardinal goes on to say that while loyalty to one's own beliefs is necessary, this does not imply that one possesses all the truth. This type of encounter calls for an attitude of humility: "It is said that between participants there must be a spirit of equality; in fact, it is truer to say, as St. Paul puts it, that each participant ought to consider his brother as his superior (Phil 2:3) since in fact he is dealing with that in him which comes from God."[14]

Cardinal Duval saw obstacles to dialogue in Algeria as coming from the identification of Christianity with its colonial past; the North-South divide with those in the developing world perceiving Christians as being on the side of the rich; and an attitude of superiority on the part of Christians.[15] Msgr. Duval was aware of the importance of what Christians and Muslims hold in common, namely, "the unity and the transcendence of God, his mercy, his omnipotence, creation, the resurrection of the dead, universal judgement."[16] One of the benefits of dialogue is that it makes Christians more acutely aware of their own central beliefs. Msgr. Duval constantly returns to the central insight of Christianity, namely, that God is love and that the best and the surest way to God is through the practice of fraternal charity: "Muslims know well that for us God is love and that Christian morality can be summed up in the practice of fraternal love. It is up to Christians to show that this love must be lived in spirit and in truth...When one is Christian, one must believe in the revolutionary power of fraternal love. If one doesn't believe in that, I ask myself what is left that is Christian in one's conscience."[17] By refusing to identify the Gospel message with a particular culture or race, Cardinal Duval won acceptance for the remnant of the Christian Church left after independence.

Fidelity to the Algerian People

His faithfulness to the Christian message was also mirrored in his faithfulness to the Algerian people. From his arrival in the country in 1947, he believed that he would live and die there. His commitment was without reserve. He was proud of his Algerian nationality and fully identified with the aspirations of the Algerian nation to make its contribution to the human family: "All my apostolate in Algeria, I can sum it up in one word: friendship. I believe in the power of friendship."[18] And indeed he had numerous Muslim and Christian friends from all strata of society. The final years of his life were to test his belief in his adopted country as Algeria was once again plunged into a cycle of fratricidal violence. The beheading of the Tibhirine monks was the final bitter cup of suffering that he had to drink shortly before his own death. He was heard to murmur, "So much suffering! But it will have to come to an end some day. Then you will see that Algeria will astound the world."[19]

On hearing of the death of the seven monks on May 23, he said to his niece, Louise, "The death of the monks has crucified me."[20] He lasted a further seven days before departing this life on May 30, 1996, at the age of 92. Fittingly, he shared his funeral mass with the seven monks of Tibhirine in his beloved Notre-Dame d'Afrique, on June 2, 1996.

PART II:

The Nineteen Martyrs

CHAPTER FOUR

The Gospel Life of Brother Henri Vergès

1930–1994

HENRI WAS THE FIRST OF nineteen religious to be assassinated by Muslim fundamentalists between 1994 and 1996. He is not an easy person to write about because his life was in many ways so ordinary. It was only extraordinary in the heroic way he lived out his vocation as a Marist brother, a vocation of humble service and availability to the Muslim youth of Algeria. Henri's life of silent witness and service became more widely known in the aftermath of his brutal assassination in the Kasbah of Algiers on Sunday, May 8, 1994. Along with Sr. Paul-Hélène, a Little Sister of the Assumption, he was gunned down at point-blank range in the library that he ran for more than one thousand disadvantaged eleventh and twelfth graders. His life had up until then been hidden from the wider public view, but it has much to teach us. In an age of increasing tension between Islam and Christianity, Br. Henri sought to understand Islam from the inside. And he also showed us how, in the light of Vatican II, the vocation of a teaching brother could retain all its relevance and apostolic vigor.

Henri was born on July 15, 1930, at Matemale, a small village in the French Pyrenees. He was the first of six children and his father worked hard as a small farmer to rear his family. At the age of twelve Henri entered the Marist brothers and in 1952 took his final vows. Henri had always cherished the idea of becoming a missionary but had never considered Algeria as a possible destination. After many unsuccessful requests to his superiors for a missionary posting, he had decided to leave the matter in God's hands. To his surprise, he was asked by his superior to join the Marist community in Algiers, a country that had never attracted him. He landed at Algiers on the feast of the Transfiguration, August 6, 1969. His challenge was to "reveal the face of Christ" to his Muslim brothers and sisters in a country undergoing the birth pangs of independence after 132 years of French domination. Not only was Algeria a country in search of an identity, but its Islamic faith was also trying to define itself in opposition to the values of the secular West. Henri was to be caught up and immersed in the fallout from these movements.

The Fifth Gospel of Our Lives

What was a Marist brother doing in a country that had overnight become a totally Muslim country with the departure of the French after independence in 1962? Henri's first assignment was to take over as headmaster in the Diocesan school of St. Bonaventure. This school had 750 pupils, five hundred of them in the primary section. The students were now totally Muslim as were most of the staff. There was a Marist community of five brothers; some of them, however, were only there on short-term contracts as coopérants doing social work in lieu of national service. Henri had no desire whatsoever to proselytize. However, he was clear that their mission in Algeria was to show forth Christ through the life of the Marist community and of each of its members. For Henri this Christian witness could help the struggling Algerian people to "hold on to its personality and to its faith in the one God."[1] Henri at no time tried to convert any of his pupils, but as an educator he sought to keep alive the authentic religious and human values that their Islamic faith had to offer. The notion of presence, a humble presence that speaks through actions rather than words was central to Henri's vision of being a missionary and educator: "So that these young people may sense through me a Presence which loves them and *which calls them* to be their best selves...Christ must shine through us. The fifth Gospel which everyone can read is the Gospel of our lives."[2]

A MAN OF PRAYER AND COMMUNITY

How did Henri go about radiating the presence of Christ to others? How did he go about preaching the fifth Gospel, the Gospel of loving witness in everyday life? Henri was a man of prayer who had absorbed the message of St. John's Gospel. In it we see Jesus' dependence on the Father, his realization that he is sent by the Father and has no message other than the message given to him by the Father. "The words that I say to you I do not speak on my own; but the Father who dwells in me does his works" (John 14:10). So it was with Henri. The words he spoke and the life he lived pointed to someone else, to an indwelling Presence at work through him. This witness was the result of a disciplined life of prayer and service. Henri prayed the office, attended mass, and set time aside for daily personal prayer, spiritual reading, and study. He was aware that any fruitfulness in his life would only come about as a result of a personal relationship with Jesus Christ.

Henri was a natural community person. He came from a family of six and had lived in Marist communities from the age of twelve. In addition, he was eminently practical—good at cooking, gardening, and working as the community handyman. His Marist brother, Marcos, who lived for nine years with him in Algeria, remarked that in all of those years Henri had done the cooking without ever complaining or asking to be replaced. Another brother, Michel, who shared his life in Algiers, remarked that

Henri had all the little virtues, "service, joy, simplicity, Marian piety, faith, dedication, humility."[3] Br. Michel, I'm sure, does not mean us to take him literally when he refers to these virtues as "little"; *unspectacular* would, perhaps, be a better rendering of what he is trying to say. Anyone experienced in community life will know how costly these virtues can be. Many years of living in community had revealed to Henri the uniqueness of each person. He wrote, "Rather than just tolerating others, we must try to find God's gift to each individual so that we can marvel at it."[4]

A Life Closer to the Poor

The first seven years of Henri's life in Algeria were spent in Algiers. In 1976 all the Catholic schools were nationalized by the Socialist government. Henri, finding himself without a job, applied with one other brother to teach within the national education system. He was given a post in a small Algerian town, Sour-El-Ghozlane, on a high plateau 120 km southeast of Algiers. Henri was pleased with this new position as it brought him closer to the ideal of Marcellin Champagnat, the founder of the Marists, who wished his teaching brothers to live a humble life close to the poor. Overnight Henri found himself no longer the headmaster of a prestigious school in the capital but instead a teacher of mathematics in a remote Algerian town of fifteen thousand people. Two years into his twelve-year stay, his companion left and Henri had to wait five years before another brother came to join him. These were years of solitude for him. He lived in a small flat on the third floor of an apartment block, truly immersed in the humble life of the Algerian people. There was no running water from June to October of each year and there were also shortages from time to time of various foodstuffs—meat was scarce and expensive and no butter was available for a whole year. Henri now lived to the full the poverty and humble life of Nazareth, which was the ideal of the Marist founder.

In his final years his life in Algiers was equally simple. Sr. Janet Hotine, an English Augustinian, who knew him then, said to me, "There was nothing in the house. He was as poor as a church mouse. Any brass farthing he had was given away to people or to the upkeep of the library. He himself led an extremely austere life."[5] In a letter at the end of January 1976 to the Provincial Chapter, Henri described his life in Sour-El-Ghozlane: "All the exterior trappings of power have disappeared: we are simple servants of everyone, without any more human security than in the past, but happy to find ourselves in the midst of a less well off population than in the capital. Our concern? To be a humble presence which witnesses to the Lord Jesus with whom we try, too imperfectly, to be in communion more and more, a presence which maintains and develops dialogue with our Algerian Muslim brothers, in a reciprocal discovery of our respective values."[6]

A Desire to Understand Each Other

What was the nature of this dialogue that Henri tried to establish with his Muslim brothers and sisters? He realized that a desire for mutual understanding is at the basis of all dialogue. For dialogue to be fruitful there was a need to understand the Muslim faith from the inside, so to speak. The indispensable tool for this was a good knowledge of Arabic and of the Qur'an, both of which he achieved. For without a solid understanding of Muslim culture and its religious values, "there cannot be any respect and without respect there cannot be any sympathy and openness."[7] Henri goes on to say that the person engaging in religious dialogue must have a profound respect for the personal freedom of others and a profound sense of the truth, along with a desire to submit to the will of God, "frankness not only towards others, but also towards oneself and

God, that is one of the most important conditions for meeting Muslims on a spiritual level."[8] As a concrete sign of his fidelity to the Algerian people and of his desire to understand their way of life, he applied, unsuccessfully, for Algerian citizenship in 1983.

As someone who took the Vatican Council seriously and studied its documents as a regular part of his spiritual life, Henri was open to the spiritual riches that Islam had to offer. His membership of the Ribat,[9] an interfaith group of Muslims and Catholics which met twice a year, stimulated his prayer and reflection. In his work, Henri was in a good position to get to know Islam from the inside, especially during the five years that he spent alone at Sour-El-Ghozlane.[10] However, he felt that a desire on the part of Muslims to understand Christianity would probably only come about as a result of their seeing Christians live out the Gospel in all its fullness. His Muslim acquaintances were attracted to Henri by his life of prayer; they sensed something of the "mystery living in him." He writes: "Deep friendships are born, flower, especially during the five years which I have to spend on my own…Sharing grows more intense and makes one sense in the mutual respect, in the admiration sometimes, the Mystery of God present even in the diversity of our religions. His Spirit is there…It is He who, on occasion, makes our hearts beat as one. A deepening for me, in this contact with the Islam of the people, of the meaning of prayer, of the sovereignty of God and of brotherly welcome."[11]

Availability in the Here and Now

After twelve years teaching in Sour-El-Ghozlane, Henri's yearly teaching contract was not renewed. Thus began the third and final stage of his twenty-five years in Algeria. He returned to Algiers to run a library and a social center in the Kasbah at 46 rue Ben Cheneb. Over one thousand eleventh and twelfth graders were members of this library, which provided them with textbooks, mainly in Arabic, and, most importantly, a place of peace and quiet in which to work. Predominantly female, these students came from disadvantaged families where space and quiet were hard to find. Henri was assisted in this work by fellow Marist, Br. Michel Voute, and by Sr. Paul-Hélène, who was to meet the same tragic fate as Henri.

One word that crops up time and time again while reading Henri's writings is *disponibilité,* or "availability." Henri had that rare spiritual gift of being totally focused and present to his evangelical service of others. This availability allowed him to serve others without any preconditions. He went where the Holy Spirit and his Order wanted him to go. It is in such availability that the charism of celibacy finds its fulfillment. One thinks especially of his five years alone in Sour-El-Ghozlane, where his sense of dedication and single-mindedness never wavered. Henri writes of a sudden moment of insight when all became clear a few months before his call to serve in Algeria: "the complete initiative must be left in the hands of the Lord, while trying without worry to discern His will in all circumstances and committing myself to it with all the potential which he has given to me. To give myself completely to living out the reality given to me in the here and now."[12] Such an attitude of availability, he writes, allows one's whole being to be filled with peace. It is a gift of the Spirit and a cause for thanksgiving.

An Authentic Witness of the Love of Christ

All foreigners had been ordered by the GIA (Armed Islamic Group) to leave Algeria by December 1, 1993, under threat of death. Friends warned Henri that his name was on the hit list of the fundamentalists. He refused to be intimidated by these threats, saying, "This risk is part of the contract." Sunday, May 8, 1994, arrived like any other morning. Because of a demonstration for peace happening in the nearby streets, there were fewer students in the library than usual. In the early afternoon three young fundamentalists entered disguised as policeman. Death came quickly for Henri and Paul-Hélène. The first youth, carrying a pistol, shot Henri once in the face and the second fired one bullet into the back of Paul-Hélène's neck. Henri collapsed, placing his hand, which he had held out to his murderer, on his chest. Twenty-five years of total dedication and service to the youth of Algeria had come to a violent and tragic end.

Henri's life and message of peace continue, however, to inspire and to give life to others. A few months before his death he wrote: "In our daily relationships, let us openly take the side of love, forgiveness; of communion in place of hatred, vengeance, and violence."[13] These words beautifully sum up Henri's life of sacrificial love as do the poignant words of the elderly Cardinal Duval spoken at the end of the funeral service: "Dear Br. Henri and the admirable Sr. Paul-Hélène have been authentic witnesses of the love of Christ, of the absolute selflessness of the Church and of fidelity to the Algerian people."[14]

Msgr. Teissier: We Were All Under Threat

The Archbishop of Algiers, Msgr. Teissier, recalled the weeks preceding Henri's assassination and his own friendship with him.[15] He was away at the synod of the African Church in Rome when the murder occurred.

The superior of the French seminary had received a message from Algiers telling him that Br. Henri Vergès had been assassinated with Sr. Paul-Hélène. I left immediately the following morning for Algiers to rejoin the community and to participate on the evening of the following day in the funeral, which took place in Notre Dame d'Afrique. The week before my departure for Rome I had been to visit the library at rue Ben Cheneb where Henri Vergès & Paul-Hélène Saint-Raymond were working, because we were all under threat since the end of October 1993. A letter had been delivered to this house where we are now [the Diocesan House] saying that all Europeans, all foreigners who hadn't left before December 1, would in effect suffer the death penalty. There had already been a number of attacks during 1993 and at the beginning of 1994. As I was a little worried I went to see Br. Henri Vergès and in answer to my inquiry he told me that almost 95 percent of the books borrowed by the students were in Arabic. I said to myself that they would perhaps respect this library as it couldn't be seen as an instrument of French cultural propaganda. Henri Vergès, who ran the library, knew Arabic and was providing the students with the means to work in Arabic. Unfortunately I was proved wrong as they returned to do away with them, calling them crusaders who were causing harm in the district— all because they were helping twelve hundred eleventh and twelfth graders to do better in their examinations.

A TIME OF FEARFUL WAITING

We were fearful that one or other of us would be targeted and attacked. In the month of November 1993 we had closed down two communities of the sisters of St. Vincent de Paul in the Oran region because they were in places where we couldn't even go to see them, given the deteriorating security situation. They were sixty kilometers from the valley of the Chélif. Around this time we had also withdrawn the resident priest at Sidi Bouabida, as he had received a threatening letter. The Trappists had received their first visit from an armed group at 8 p.m. on Christmas Eve, 1993. Twelve Croatians working a few kilometers from the Tibhirine monastery had been beheaded or had their throats cut on December 14, 1993. Therefore we were well aware that violence was around. But we didn't know on whom it would fall. And we couldn't close down all our centers of presence because it was precisely the aim of the extremists who were attacking us to make us leave. Once the attacks had occurred it was easy to say that one should have withdrawn from that area.

I WAS DEEPLY AFFECTED

We were aware of the possibility of being assassinated since the beginning of December as I had received in this very house a threatening letter. From October 29, 1993, we knew that they intended to specially target foreigners or Christians. In truth we knew this already from the month of September 1993, when an armed group entered the house of German aid workers who were looking after the farm of the Mercedes Company. They told them that they wanted to see no more Christians in the country and that if they wanted to continue working here they had to become Muslims. Therefore we were expecting them to attack someone or other. Our two friends of Ben Cheneb were the ones targeted. Obviously I was deeply affected as I knew Henri Vergès very well. He spent many hours sitting on the couch over there. When he was at Sour-El-Ghozlane we often discussed how he might find another brother to join him there. And indeed Br. Jesús did join him for a time. Then when arabization took away his job he came to discuss what new form his commitment might take. Finally it was here that we decided together that he would take over the management of the library for the eleventh and twelfth graders which the White Fathers were about to give up.

MY MEMORY OF BR. HENRI

He was a man who gave himself fully to whatever he was doing; he gave himself fully to his responsibilities, to his prayer, to preparing his classes, to his relationships at Sour-El-Ghozlane. Later in the Kasbah, he was someone who lived a life of integrity and total fidelity. He was the first victim of the violence and he was certainly someone who had shown the greatest daily fidelity in all areas of his life. In the Kasbah he was at the service of these young eleventh and twelfth graders. Therefore the reaction to the news of his assassination tended to be, "It is the best who are struck down."

He belonged as you know to the Islamo-Christian spirituality group Le Ribat. He worked hard at improving his Arabic. He did everything with the maximum of fidelity.

CHAPTER FIVE

Six Lives Given,
Six Lives Shared

The Fidelity of Daily Life

THE WITNESS OF THE ALGERIAN martyrs in the 1990s is so
powerful because it speaks of nineteen lives given for others out
of love. And love is something that is easy to recognize but hard to
find. These nineteen martyrs, all members of religious orders,
didn't stumble into martyrdom, but knowingly assumed it out of
love for their Muslim brothers and sisters, out of solidarity with
them in their suffering. Archbishop Teissier points out that what
was peculiar to these Algerian martyrs was that they had sacrificed
their lives "not so as to avoid renouncing directly their faith, nor
to defend a Christian community, but through fidelity to a Muslim
people."[1] They were martyrs of charity in that they didn't give
their lives to defend their faith but out of love for their Muslim
brothers and sisters.

What is also striking about the death of the six sisters who
were killed is that all of them, except for Sr. Paul-Hélène, were
either on their way to mass or returning from it. Little did their
assassins know how appropriate their timing was. As did Jesus in
the Eucharist, each one of the sisters gave her life freely out of love
for the people she served. And like Jesus, each one of the sisters
was innocent of any wrongdoing.

Love of the Algerian People

Each of the sisters knew that by choosing to remain in Algeria they were putting their lives on the line. And the motivation for this hard and difficult choice was their love for the Algerian people, their Muslim brothers and sisters, a love based on the Gospel. They were living out what Jesus had taught them, "For this reason the Father loves me, because I lay down my life in order to take it up again. No one takes it from me, but I lay it down of my own accord...No one has greater love than this, to lay down one's life for one's friends" (John 10:17–18; 15:13).

These religious were well known to their Muslim neighbors because they had shared their lives with them, living in the working-class districts and serving the neediest sections of the population. All of the sisters were involved in ministering to the people as nurses, librarians, or domestic science teachers. This apostolic witness was the fruit of dedicated lives of prayer and community living. Living in a Muslim country where people are called publicly to prayer five times a day, the Christian religious would have made no impact if they weren't clearly seen to be people of prayer. The sisters were known in their districts as "women of God." There was no dichotomy between their service of others and their love of God. The sisters didn't allow their apostolic service to become detached from its source of fruitfulness, the Father's love for them.

Friendship with the People

Practically all of the foreign nationals had left the country by 1994 as a result of the threat of execution by the fundamentalists. The religious who remained behind were all too obvious as there were no other foreigners left in the country. Sr. Odette in her last Christmas letter remarked how people looked at her with amazement in the streets of Algiers and showed their appreciation of her presence by many little gestures. An anonymous passerby offered her a rose; another gave her a bag of croissants. The bus driver noticing where she was going would specially stop to ensure that her journey home would be as safe as possible. It was through living side by side and sharing in the everyday life of the people that these religious overcame any barriers of suspicion and mutual incomprehension.

And this was probably the main reason why they were targeted by the fundamentalists. I suspect it was not the difference of religion and race that offended the extremists so much as their friendship with the people. They had broken down the barriers of prejudice and exclusion on which fundamentalism thrives. For their witness to our common humanity they were put to death. Their friendship with the Algerian people witnessed to the common Fatherhood of God which is shared by Christians and Muslims, a fatherhood that makes us brothers and sisters.

Sr. Paul-Hélène[2]

The first of the sisters to be assassinated was Sr. Paul-Hélène Saint-Raymond, a Little Sister of the Assumption. In the early afternoon of May 8, 1994, two fundamentalists disguised as policemen fatally wounded Paul-Hélène and Henri Vergès as they welcomed students to the library they ran for eleventh and twelfth graders in the Kasbah, the poorest area of Algiers. Ironically, at the same time a march for peace was taking place on the sea-front in the center of the town.

Paul-Hélène came eighth in a family of ten children and had spent twenty-two years in Algeria, first as a nursing sister, then as a family social worker, and finally as an assistant in the library. She had a determined and energetic character that she wholeheartedly consecrated to helping the needy people for whom she worked. Her work had nothing spectacular about it—it was a question of being present, of sharing in the everyday joys and sorrows of a suffering people. She had a very determined personality, and at times her religious sisters found this single-mindedness difficult to live with. Père Bonnamour, her parish priest, told me that on arrival in heaven, her first question to God would be, "But why did you do it *that* way?"

The defenseless Paul-Hélène was gunned down at point-blank range. Msgr. Teissier recalled Sr. Paul-Hélène in an interview with me:

She was the sister of one of my fellow seminarians. That was a first point of contact. I was concerned because she traveled on foot from Belcourt, in the center of town where she lived, to Ben Cheneb right over in the east end of Algiers. But we weren't sure which was the more dangerous—the bus or on foot—as there were also people being killed on the bus and also cars were being booby trapped and set off as buses went by. That very day, May 8, had been a day of demonstrations by liberal movements against Islamism. Among those who were injured when a grenade was thrown at the marchers was Mme Khalida, the minister for culture, whom I knew well and who was a guest here from time to time.

I asked Msgr. Teissier how well he knew Sr. Paul-Hélène and he said:

I knew her well as we are only a small Church and we all know each other. Sr. Paul-Hélène had spirit. She chose what she wanted to do and she did it. That's why she went on foot from Belcourt to the library even after the violence had started. Unfortunately after the attack against her, the other sisters of her congregation, apart from Sr. Geneviève, decided that they could no longer remain in this insecure environment. One sister wanted me to close down all the religious communities. I replied that the Church must remain faithful to the Algerian people. Of course, we would support those who wished to leave and we would also support the decision of those who wished to stay.

After these first two assassinations, Msgr. Teissier and the Christian community were heartened by the support that they received from their Muslim friends. Among many letters of support, a journalist and a university teacher wrote: "Once more, unlike the assassins we say to you; here is your home, we love you and we pray by your side for the repose of the soul of those who have been slaughtered in such a cowardly manner."[3]

Sisters Esther and Caridad

In the working-class district of Bab-el-Oued, Algiers, three Spanish Augustinian Missionary Sisters—Esther Paniagua Alonso, Caridad Alvarez Martín, and Lourdès Miguelez—were much loved by their Algerian neighbors. There had originally been four sisters, but the previous July Sr. Monserrat had gone back to Spain to become novice mistress. Esther and Lourdès worked as nurses in the state hospital system, while Caridad looked after the house. Esther worked in a reeducation center for handicapped children. She was a reserved person and difficult to get to know. Caridad was more outgoing. Sr. Janet Hotine, who has lived in Algeria for a long time, knew her well. In an interview with me she recalled Sister Caridad:

> Caridad was a very warm-hearted homemaker. She did the cooking and looked after the house. She would have been a great Spanish mum. Shortly before her assassination I ran up behind her and touched her shoulder in the market. She

hadn't seen me approach and she jumped in shock. I'm sure she sensed that the end was near. She told me that two young girls had come to the door, rung the bell, and asked if they could rent a room. Caridad said, "But we don't let out rooms." And they replied, insistently, "But you're going to leave very soon, aren't you?" Caridad looked very white as she said this and later we thought it must have been a kind of warning, a hint from someone that something was being planned.

The Word of God Lit up Each Day

An Algerian Christian who knew the sisters well had this to say: "Esther was a nurse in a hospital and she couldn't just walk out. She was a brilliant nurse. One of her Algerian colleagues begged her to leave but she couldn't. We didn't talk about the situation. We lived with it. The Lord was the one with whom we discussed it. The only thing we said to each other was, 'Be careful.'" All three, after a lengthy period of community discernment, had chosen to stay in solidarity with their suffering neighbors. It was Sunday, October 23, 1994, Mission Sunday, a few months after the assassination of Br. Henri and Sr. Paul-Hélène. The sisters had been joined by their Provincial for a visitation. That very day the Spanish ambassador visited Esther at the hospital and tried to persuade her to leave Bab-el-Oued. She had replied, "God is everywhere, even in Bab-el-Oued." On that final day Caridad in her talk with the Provincial had said, "when one discovers the true meaning of mission, one is fulfilled."[4] The time for the Sunday Eucharist had arrived and they left separately in pairs as a security precaution. Esther and Caridad had just rung the bell of the apartment where mass was to be celebrated. When Sr. Marie-Danièle, a Little Sister of Charles de Foucauld opened the door, Esther and Caridad were on the pavement, dying, and beyond help.

Sr. Lourdès was one of the four sisters who set out for mass on that fateful day. More than ten years later on April 3, 2006, she spoke to me about their life before the assassinations:

We are a closely knit church here. It's our great wealth. Everyone knows each other and helps each other out. Here one is known; one is a person. The Eucharist helped us enormously to carry the suffering of the people and to see clearly. The Word of God illuminated each day. We felt God's presence among us. We were very cheerful. The first two deaths hit us very hard. We started the Eucharist for Henri and Paul-Hélène in a very sombre mood and then we were overcome by joy. The parents of Henri Vergès said to us, "Your love for one another is obvious."

WHEN WILL THE KILLING END?

The Superior General had come to visit us just before the assassinations. As she left she said to us, "I feel very afraid for you." As the three of us and the Provincial set out for mass I remarked, "The four of us should not go together. If we must be killed, let them kill two of us, not all four." Esther and Caridad went ahead and had turned the corner just before the apartment of the sisters of Charles de Foucauld where mass was going to be celebrated. We heard the shots very clearly. People were running about in all directions. I said, "It's our sisters. Let's go and see what's happened." Some youths told us to go no further. I then asked them what had happened. They told us that some foreigners had been fired at. I knew that it must have been our sisters because they had been just ahead of us. We then took refuge in the house of some Algerian neighbors who wouldn't let us go outside. With the arrival of the police we went to the scene of the crime. Cari was put in the ambulance. Esther was lying there on the ground. She too was put in the ambulance. At the same time Fr. Louis Fontugne was cleansing the pavement of the blood, blood shed for the Algerian people. After telephoning the Spanish Embassy, we left for the hospital with the police. Msgr. Teissier arrived very quickly. A half an hour later Esther was dead. Cari was transferred to the military hospital where there were better facilities. One of the doctors was in a half-crazed state and was shouting, "When will the killing end? We no longer know where to put the corpses!" The bullet had lodged in Cari's head. The 10 p.m. curfew forced us to leave and we went to the Spanish Embassy. At 9:45 a.m. the doctor came to tell us that Cari was dead.

WE WERE CARRYING THE CROSS WITH JESUS

The ambassador's wife had put a huge cross on a crystal table in our bedroom. It was then that we began to cry. We understood that we were carrying the cross with Jesus, the cross which is the sign of the free gift of our lives given to this people.

During the crisis we couldn't go out much. We had more time for prayer, to prepare for this event. We celebrated the Eucharist where we carried the cross of the people, their suffering. We have been welcomed into the house of Islam. To celebrate the Eucharist—Jesus died for everyone—is a gift of life for them also. A life given, a life shared, that's what the Eucharist is. By staying with the people we had freely offered our lives out of love for them. On my return, after eight year's absence, in 2002, people were crying and said to me, "Lourdès, your return is the very best gift which you could give us." And the doctor said to me, "The best witness is that you have forgiven us, that you love us." Others asked me why I had returned to share their misery. I replied, "I love you and I want to share your life." They find it difficult to believe that I am not here to convert them.

The Algerian journalist, Saïd Mekbel, paid them this homage in the newspaper *Le Matin* on October 27, 1994: "They were two women on their way to God to ask forgiveness. They were undoubtedly offering up their little prayers for us, unfortunate Algerians, oppressed by the scourge [of violence]. Perhaps we will be lacking for a long time the final prayers of these two religious who wished to tip the scales in favor of peace and mercy. Towards what world of darkness will we now plunge, we who only dream of light."[5] Shortly afterward on December 4, like numerous other journalists, Saïd Mekbel was in his turn assassinated by the fundamentalists.

Msgr. Tessier spoke to me about the fates of Sisters Esther and Caridad:

I felt this attack very deeply because two weeks beforehand in this very house we completed two-and-a-half days of discernment with the superior general of this congregation, a Brazilian, who had come from Rome, and with the provincial, María Jesús, a Spaniard who had come from Madrid. I led the reflection on what was the meaning of our commitment here, what was our work. I remember in particular that I led a reflection based on the Annunciation. These texts were published afterwards. All the sisters decided to remain and even to stay in the Bab-el-Oued district. We said to them that they could continue their work in Algeria, but that they should move to a less working-class, dangerous district. They said, "This is the district where we are known, this is the district where we must remain."

I had often met Sr. Esther because she had studied Arabic for two years at the PISAI (The Pontifical Institute for Islamic & Arabic Studies) in Rome. Even though the

Augustinian Missionary Sisters have been present in Algeria for fifty years, she was the first sister of her order to be properly trained in Arabic at the PISAI. Consequently, I was impressed by the commitment of this sister who after two years of learning Arabic had returned to Algeria to take up nursing again. By temperament she was fairly calm, fairly reserved, fairly discreet, very committed to her work as a nurse. She trained as a nurse in Algeria and was working for an Algerian professor whom I knew well, professor Assela.

I knew Sr. Caridad less well because she stayed at home to look after the house. On Sunday, October 23, I had gone to visit a politically active Algerian lady, Mme. Aslaoui, whom I knew well and whose husband had been assassinated. While there I also offered my condolences to the father of the assassinated man, who lived in Bologhine [a suburb of Algiers near Bab-el-Oued]. Afterwards I decided to visit Cardinal Duval, who lived nearby, to see how he felt about the developing situation. On my arrival at his door I rang the bell and it was opened by his niece who looked very troubled. She said, "We've just received a telephone call to say that the two sisters, Esther and Caridad, have been assassinated." I immediately went down to Bab-el-Oued to join them but their bodies had already been taken to the local hospital. From that hospital I left in an ambulance for the military hospital of Aïn Naadja where for a few hours there was some hope that one of the sisters might survive. But she died during the night.

Sisters Angèle-Marie and Bibiane

The next two sisters to be slain, Angèle-Marie Jeanne Littlejohn born in Tunis in 1933 and Bibiane Denise Leclercq born in Gazerau,

France, in 1930, were on their way home from mass. It was September 3, 1995, eleven months after the death of Esther and Caridad. Angèle-Marie and Bibiane belonged to the congregation of Our Lady of the Apostles. There were three sisters in their community in Belcourt where they had run a dressmaking school since 1964 for the girls of this working-class suburb of Algiers. As they visited all the families of the girls whom they taught, they were well known and much loved in the district. Not so long before their deaths, a local victorious football team had assembled in front of the sisters' balcony to show off their trophy to them.

In 1964 the parish priest of Belcourt, Fr. Scotto, asked the Sisters of Our Lady of the Apostles to help a local voluntary organization that was providing literacy education in the area. Sisters Bibiane and Angèle-Marie were sent (to be later joined by Sr. Yolanda) and remained in Belcourt until their assassination thirty-one years later. They later ran a dressmaking school for teenage girls who had dropped out of school. They knew everybody, especially the poorest, and they weren't afraid to visit even the most deprived areas. From 1969 to 1970 the municipality took over the running of these courses and the sisters were from then on their employees.

They Wanted Only the Best for Them

Fr. Pierre Lafitte, who lives in Belcourt, spoke to me about the selfless work of Sisters Angèle-Mary and Bibiane:

> The sisters showed their affection for their pupils through the high standards which they expected of them. They had confidence in their capacity to create works of beauty. They wanted only the best for them, that they should succeed in life. They were saying to them, "You have got worth because you are capable of creating works of qual-

ity." They gave them pride in themselves. This was a work of salvation as these girls had experienced failure at school and felt useless. They didn't convert the girls whom they taught but they did bring them salvation!

Fr. Bonnamour, their parish priest at Belcourt, also knew the three sisters very well and described their presence to me with admiration and affection:

Bibiane was completely devoted to her work. She was very attached to her vocation and to her work and had excellent relationships with her pupils. She had the capacity to give herself totally to her work. Angèle-Marie was a first-class embroiderer and was very creative. They set very high standards for their pupils and worked themselves to the bone for them. The sisters respected the religion of their pupils. They did their work with absolute respect for others.

The sisters were constantly aware of the possibility of being killed. They had no problem about death. Death did not frighten them. They had a living faith before death. They had served the locality so well that everyone loved and respected them, even the Islamists, who would also say, "Sisters, pray for us." They had a wonderful influence.

Fear Reigned

At the time of the killing of the sisters, Islamist violence was at its height and fear reigned, especially in the working-class suburbs of Algiers. Fr. Lafitte himself was spared this slow death that an all-enveloping fear can bring. In his own words: "I wasn't afraid. I didn't even have courage. Being courageous is to overcome fear." However, this gift wasn't given to everyone. Despite the fact that the sisters were universally loved and admired in Belcourt, people were too frightened to show their support after their deaths. Père Lafitte had to move their belongings with only the help of two religious, one of them elderly. There was only one elderly woman from the area who had the courage to help them. At their funeral there weren't even ten Algerians. Everyone was terrified of the consequences of being seen to oppose the Islamists. An Algerian Christian told me of a person who was assassinated in the market at Bab-el-Oued and of someone who stooped down to help him. The next day that person was killed. "You had to leave people to die. A neighbor was killed and another neighbor saw that he wasn't dead and came to recite the Shahada so that he wouldn't go to hell. The following day the neighbor was killed. Seemingly, he should have allowed him to go to hell."

An assassin's bullet took the sisters' lives within sight of their apartment as they were returning from mass. Their participation in Jesus' self-offering on our behalf was now complete. Sr. Bibiane had a quotation from Dietrich Bonhoeffer among her personal papers, "To be with and for others in freedom, gratuitousness and joy, even to the gift of one's life and afterwards to return to the Father, consummated."[6]

Msgr. Tessier described to me how he learned about the deaths of Angèle-Marie and Bibiane:

> It was Pierre Lafitte who told me. He lived in the same district as the sisters, in Belcourt. He had been informed by Fr. Bonnamour. I went straight away with Fr. Lafitte to the scene but the bodies of our sisters had been taken to another hospital. We went to several hospitals looking for them before finding out that they had been taken to the mortuary of St. Genès' cemetery. So we had at first wandered about the streets of Algiers and in the various hospitals trying to find their bodies. As bishop I visit everybody and I had often visited them in their second floor flat in Belcourt where they taught dressmaking to

young Algerian girls. They were totally committed to the service of these girls and very well known in the district. They went about the district thinking that their lives would be respected as everyone knew they were working for the good of the girls of the area. I don't think that they were expecting to be attacked. A little while before that they had said to me, "As for us, everyone knows us." It was at the start of Islamism. We hadn't realized how barbaric it would become. Many still believed that their work, their commitment to the service of the poorest, would protect them from the violence.

According to Fr. Belaïd, the Algerians felt humiliated by the killing of the religious. Msgr. Tessier told me why they felt this way: "Because they were aware that the people who had been struck down were innocent and were working for the good of the people."

Sister Odette

Two more sisters, Odette and Chantal, Little Sisters of the Sacred Heart, were next on the assassins' list. Fortunately this time there was a survivor, Sr. Chantal. Odette worked at the Diocesan study center, *Les Glycines,* in Algiers. The community of three lived in Appreval, a suburb of Algiers adjacent to Kouba, noted for its fundamentalist fervor. Odette, who had been a primary school teacher in France, spent her evenings helping the children of the area with their homework. In a letter home she wrote that, while recognizing the high-risk nature of her work, she tried to live as normal a life as possible so as "to resist through solidarity" the enveloping violence and chaos, to show through their presence that "one can live fraternally with difference."

She Knew She Was Going to Die

Sr. Janet, who knew Odette well, told me of her two great loves, gardening and gathering together the neighborhood children. She would sit them down with her homemade yogurts to make sure that they had enough protein to grow. She would also help them with their homework and play games with them. There was always a gang of them in the kitchen. An Algerian Christian with whom I spoke recalled Sister Odette fondly:

> She was really devoted to what she was doing. She would give her time freely. People wouldn't notice her presence she was so discreet but yet she knew what people needed and would do it for them without any fuss. She did it naturally. I think she knew she was going to die. Three days before she was assassinated I said hello to her. She said, "I want a kiss." Laughing, I said "No, I'll come back tomorrow." She said, "Tomorrow might be too late." That was Wednesday and she was assassinated on Friday. She sensed that she was going to go. She never looked unhappy but she looked very serious at this time.

Sr. Janet added: "The Lord gave every single person who went time to get ready. I did feel there was a question mark over my own life. One has to walk beyond fear. One can only do it face to face with the Lord. I said, 'If it's now, Lord, you won't get a very good bargain. You can see I'm not ready to go. But it's up to you to decide.' A lot of Algerians live beyond worry and fear. There are so many imponderables. You can't do anything about it."

Odette purposely decided to remain in Algeria in order "to be Christ's own presence." She understood her decision to stay in the light of the Eucharist—Jesus' self-offering on our behalf. Friday, November 10, 1995, was the day appointed for her own offering. Chantal, though wounded twice, survived. Odette died on the spot. The previous summer on holiday in France, as she took leave of her sister-in-law, Odette's parting words to her were, "Since you wish to give me a present for my return to Algeria, let it be your acceptance of the fact that I may have to give my life for my Algerian brothers."[7]

Putting Nothing Before Christ

Perhaps what is most moving about these Sisters' witness is their single-mindedness, which is at the heart of the Gospel invitation to put nothing before Christ. Their Algerian neighbors and their superiors recognized in them people whose lives were truly given, both to the Lord and to the service of their Algerian brothers and sisters.

The witness of the Algerian martyrs speaks in a special way to the Church at the start of a new century. Many commentators think that the big challenge for Christianity in the twenty-first century will be to find a way of peacefully coexisting with a more militant and fundamentalist Islam. These martyrs point the way forward for us. As Archbishop Teissier has noted, these Christians assumed martyrdom not to defend their faith as such but to show solidarity with the suffering Muslim people of Algeria. And these acts of sacrificial love have greatly deepened Muslim-Christian understanding in that country. As the sisters so well understood, it is in the Eucharist that we learn how to share our lives and offer them for others.

CHAPTER SIX

Strength in Weakness

The White Fathers of Tizi-Ouzou

JEAN FISSET, AN ELDERLY WHITE FATHER, was deeply moved by the funeral of his assassinated brothers in Tizi-Ouzou:

> Like Jesus, I was overwhelmed and I turned towards the Father, giving thanks during the burial of my brothers, the four victims of Tizi-Ouzou. [I recall] the closed shops along the route of the funeral cortège, and the silent crowd who joined it as far as the cemetery. Imagine...four Christian missionaries led to their resting place by a crowd of [about 4,000] Muslims; and even more, on entering the cemetery, this crowd emitting *youyous* and applauding as if for their own martyrs.
>
> Msgr. Teissier, before all those present, was able to find the words which expressed fully the meaning of this demonstration by affirming: "The Mission of the Church is to find and raise up brothers." That's exactly, it seems to me, what this gathering expressed, a witness to a love which had been recognized and shared. This moment will remain the summit of my missionary life, a luminous memory until the end of my existence.[1]

On December 27, 1994, it was the turn of four of the White Fathers in Tizi-Ouzou to suffer a brutal ending. About midday six armed men disguised as policemen made their appearance at the gate of the house that, during the day, was open for anyone to enter. Four of the men entered the courtyard and locked up those working on the construction of a new library and those who had come to seek help from Fr. Jean Chevillard. Fr. Jean, aware that these weren't policemen from the town, tried to resist and to raise the alarm. He was shot five times at point blank range, once directly into the heart. The other three priests, attempting to escape, were likewise killed before they could reach the gate. It is possible that the fundamentalists were hoping to kidnap the four priests as a reprisal for the killing of four Islamists who had hijacked an Air France plane at Algiers airport a few days earlier on December 24.

The Glory of God

Martyrdom has always held a fascination for Christians as the closest conformity to the life of Jesus and to his death on the cross. Thus the day after Christmas we celebrate the death of the first martyr, Stephen. We are told that Stephen "gazed into heaven and saw the glory of God" (Acts 7:55). The martyr wishes to participate in the "glory of God" through a close identification with the sacrificial death of Jesus who gave his life that others might live. It was the irresistible pull of this "spirit of glory" (1 Pet 4:14), this sharing in Christ's suffering, which from the start attracted the candidates who joined the Missionaries of Africa, better known as the White Fathers, founded in 1868 in Algiers by Cardinal Lavigerie. One of the first candidates who sought admission to the novitiate had his papers signed by the Cardinal, *Visum pro martyrio,* "authorized for martyrdom." Lavigerie had no illusions about the difficulties facing those who joined his missionary society: "I can only offer poverty, abnegation, the perils of a land almost unknown and until now impenetrable, and at the end of it all, perhaps the death of a martyr."[2] Martyrdom has been part of the challenge that has faced the White Fathers since the beginning of the Society. In the first thirteen years of the Society, ten White Fathers were killed and six more met their deaths as a result of exhaustion.

Alain Dieulangard

What motivated the most recent of the martyred White Fathers in their service of the Algerian Church and people? Alain Dieulangard, aged 75, was the eldest of those slain. He was born on May 21, 1919, in Brittany, one of ten children, five of whom became religious. His studies were interrupted by the Second World War and after demobilization he obtained a bachelor's degree in law at Rennes. He then joined the White Fathers and was ordained a priest at Carthage in 1950. He wanted to go as a missionary to Uganda but providence decided otherwise, and after studying Arabic for two years in Tunis he was posted to Kabylia in Algeria. Reserved and endowed with a good sense of humor, Alain was known affectionately, even when young, as *grand-père,* grandfather, in recognition of his wisdom. In all, he spent a total of forty-four years in Kabylia, during which time he mastered the language.

Alain was a born pastor who knew how to listen to the joys and sorrows of those Christians and Muslims whom he met as he traveled around Kabylia visiting his scattered parishioners. With the nationalization of the Church's schools and various institutions in 1976, Alain felt the attraction of a more silent and contemplative lifestyle. He also thought that a more contemplative approach would suit the new way of being present, which the changed circumstances now demanded of the White Fathers in Algeria. He spent six months in solitude and silence at Vénasque in France but his superior discouraged his wish to prolong this experience.

Alain's service of others was rooted in a real, living relationship with the Father. Writing to a friend after the assassination of Br. Henri and Sr. Paul-Hélène, he remarked: "The future? It is in the hands of God. I hope that we will continue at least to assure a minimum presence in the Church until peace returns, which will eventually happen."[3] Eric Bladt, who had lived with Fr. Alain at Tizi-Ouzou, summed up the good pastor this way: "He put a lot of love into whatever he did."[4] His only motivation had been to serve the Algerian people as an expression of his love for Christ.

Charles Deckers

Charles Deckers, born in Anvers, Belgium, on December 26, 1924, was one of nine children. Ordained for the White Fathers in 1950, Charlie was to spend a total of twenty-one years in Kabylia. While valuing the study of the language and culture, he also greatly appreciated personal contact and relationships as a means of getting to know a people. By 1955 he had set up a youth hostel and a Center for Professional Training for young people in Tizi-Ouzou. As a result of his closeness to the Berbers and his support for their culture and language, he fell foul of the local government and in 1976, despite having obtained Algerian nationality, he was forbidden to live in the *wilaya* or county of Tizi-Ouzou. In 1977, after a short stay in Algiers, he was put in charge of a center for Christian/Muslim dialogue, *El Kalima,* in Brussels. His genius for forming relationships led him to become involved in helping out North Africans who were in trouble. From there, in 1982, he went to work in the Yemen for five years with the Catholic Relief Service. His total availability was especially appreciated by Mother Teresa's Missionaries of Charity. Each week he made a long four- to five-hour bus journey in order to say mass for them. In 1987 he returned to Algeria to be chaplain at Notre-Dame d'Afrique in Algiers, where he welcomed pilgrims to the Basilica, the majority of whom were now Muslims. He also said daily mass at 6:30 a.m. for the Poor Clares and was constantly at the service of people in trouble, whether they were illegal African immigrants or old ladies who needed a lift up the hill to the Basilica.

On December 26, 1994, he reluctantly agreed to a community celebration of his seventieth birthday. The following day was to be his last. He had also hoped to have a second celebration the following day in Tizi-Ouzou, the feast day of his good friend, Jean Chevillard, a member of the Tizi-Ouzou community. As usual the day started with mass for the Poor Clares. The nuns remarked on the special fervor with which he said his final mass, "At the moment of elevating the host, it seemed as if he wished to become part of it."[5] And, of course, Charlie's life of generosity and service had its source and fulfillment in the life of Jesus, a life freely given for others. Earlier that year, on March 26, he had written to his family, "More than ever, I think that acts speak louder than words, even if the acts are no more than a presence, remaining on with the people. I place my fate in the hands of the Lord."[6] This witness did not go unnoticed by his Muslim friends, one of whom wrote from Oran after his death: "We are touched to the very depths of our being by the loss of a great friend, a friend of whom we can never say often enough how much we admired him for all his virtues: his nobility, his generosity, his tolerance. This friend was Fr. Deckers, a servant of the humble who loved passionately this land of Algeria."[7] He had scarcely reached Tizi-Ouzou when those who were to take his life arrived to do their bloody deed.

Jean Chevillard

Jean Chevillard, like Alain and Charlie, also came from a large family. He was born in Angers on August 27, 1925, the sixth of fifteen children. He entered the White Fathers at the age of sixteen and was ordained a priest in 1950. He was a person with first-class organizational and people skills. These skills would later be put to good use in his role as director of a center for professional training for young people, *El-Harrach,* on the outskirts of Algiers. The enrollment in this center peaked at 525 students, including 350 boarders. These same talents led to his appointment as Bursar for the White Fathers in Algeria and as Assistant Superior in France and Superior in Algeria. In 1985, he was happy to be sent to Tizi-Ouzou. He commented, "This is a community that prays."[8]

One of his jobs involved helping people with social benefits claims and other bureaucratic procedures. His tenacity and quick temper were both useful assets, as was his playful sense of humour. Great perseverance was needed to overcome official inertia in many of the cases that he had to untangle. One year after the death of Jean a beautiful tribute arrived in the post from someone who had known him more than thirty years earlier. The letter writer, as a young Muslim, had met Jean on his release from a detention camp in 1959 and was then full of hate, not unlike those young people who were later to take Jean's life. He wrote:

> Fr. Jean did not make me a Christian but he led me to God without taking me by the hand, without speaking to me in language used by religious people. It was enough for me to watch him live and to meditate on his conduct to be convinced that God's banner is one, whatever the color which people here or there may give it, and I was able to exorcise the evil which possessed me. My reason and my youthful heart gave way before this uprightness and this extreme goodness which I didn't think existed among the others. For all these last thirty years, his luminous and all so peaceful gaze has never been far from my mind.[9]

Fr. Jean had indeed witnessed both in his life and in his death to the love of Christ.

Christian Chessel

Christian Chessel was the youngest of the four assassinated White Fathers. He was born in Digne in the French Alps on October 27, 1958, and he was regarded as someone of great promise. With degrees in civil engineering and French, he was of an academic bent and enjoyed study. He first came to know Africa while completing his national service as a teacher of mathematics in the Ivory Coast. After two years in the Avignon interdiocesan seminary, he decided that his vocation lay with the White Fathers, whom he joined in 1985. In 1986, at the age of twenty-eight, he was sent to Tizi-Ouzou as part of his formation. There he immersed himself for two years in the study of the Berber language and culture and also followed a course in engineering at the university as a means of getting to know the students. Three years of theological studies at Totteridge in England followed. Finally, he spent two years in Rome studying Islam and its language. In August 1993 he joined the community in Tizi-Ouzou and was appointed superior there in June 1994.

Christian settled in to community life at Tizi-Ouzou with ease. He related well with others, and his sensitivity and sense of dedication made him well suited to the role of superior. He led a disciplined, studious existence, and his engineering background was reflected in his orderly lifestyle. His room was divided into three sections: one corner was a prayer space; another part was his office, filled with books and his inseparable companion, the computer; and finally there was his bed, also covered with books. Fr. Raphael Deillon remarked that Christian was able to lead a highly disciplined and organized life and yet at the same time he was nearly always smiling and available to others.[10] Christian was aware of his academic bent and of its possible disadvantages. In writing to Christian de Chergé to request membership of the Ribat es-Salam,[11] a Christian-Muslim interfaith group devoted to dialogue through prayer and friendship, he commented: "I have an intellectual, abstract approach to things; I feel the need to achieve a greater equilibrium by developing a more spiritual dimension, something more simple and experiential."[12] He had been preparing to build a library for students and had just received the green light to start the building from the authorities on the very morning of his assassination.

A Humble and Hidden Presence

Christian was seen as the future of the White Fathers in Algeria, that is to say, he was young, thirty-six, a man of prayer and an intellectual, the sort of person who could find new ways of incarnating the charism of the White Fathers in a changing Algeria. All the power bases of the Church had been effectively taken away with the mass departure of the French in 1962, and the final blow fell when the remaining institutions of the Church were nationalized in 1976. The White Fathers and the Church of Algeria were now called to a more humble and hidden presence, bereft of the symbols of power and status. In the words of the White Father, Armand Duval, they were being called to lead a "much simpler life: prayer, fraternal service, availability to all...Since the Spirit works in all, the witness of an authentic Christian life will help the inhabitants of the country to respond themselves to the promptings of the Spirit of God in their hearts."[13]

It was this challenge of giving "the witness of an authentic Christian life" that Christian was struggling with in his writings and life. A few months before his assassination, he wrote *La Mission Dans La Faiblesse* ("Mission in Weakness"). Perhaps the key point Christian made in relation to the position of the Christian community in Algeria, powerless and beset by violence, is contained in this insight: "To thus learn our powerlessness and to become aware of our radical poverty, of our being before God, can only be an invitation, an urgent appeal to create with others relationships not based on power; having learnt to recognize my weakness, I can not only accept that of others but see there a call to carry it, to make it mine, in imitation of Christ." This, writes Christian, will completely change the Christian community's approach to mission. In their relationships with "the other," not only will Christians refuse to impose themselves by force, but they will respond to the weakness of the other with "a greater call to love." Nor will they be afraid of the strength of the other, because they will approach them with the strength of their own weakness, a strength that comes from God alone. This weakness can very easily be misunderstood unless it is seen in the context of Christ's life of humility and service, "rooted in the strength of the paschal mystery and in the strength the Spirit. Far from being an attitude of passivity or resignation, it requires a lot of courage and demands a commitment to justice and truth, denouncing the illusory seduction of force and power."[14] This chosen weakness, in imitation of Christ, allows Christians in St Paul's words "to become all things to all people, so that [they] might by all means save some" (1 Cor 9:22).

A More Evangelical Witness

Christian was facing the difficult question that keeps coming up in the contemporary Church in Algeria and which, of course, was equally alive for Cardinal Lavigerie and Charles de Foucauld in their time: How does a Christian live out his beliefs in a Muslim society? What does the Gospel have to say to a Muslim culture? And perhaps the new issue that Christian, Msgr. Teissier, and others are grappling with, namely, the structural powerlessness of the Church. Paradoxically, this powerlessness, painful as it has been for the Church in Algeria, reflects more closely the message of the Gospel.

Msgr. Claude Rault, a former Provincial of the White Fathers in Algeria and now Bishop of Laghouat, also in Algeria, has also deeply pondered the questions raised by the powerlessness of the Church. He sees the mission of the White Fathers and of the Church in Algeria as less a matter of doing things and having big institutions and more a matter of being with the people. What the local people missed most of all after the assassination of the four White Fathers was not so much their works as their presence: "the Mission is first of all a certain quality of being. A certain quality of being present to God and to people....the Mission will be more concerned with relationships, closeness, the quality of being."[15]

This new approach or emphasis on encounter, what the Church in Algeria calls the sacrament of encounter, is much more demanding of the missionary, as the quality of his own life becomes the key to the proclamation of the Gospel. In the past, the sacraments worked regardless of the person administering them. Now the sacrament of encounter depends on the person's closeness to God, on him being a clear medium through which the love of God is passed on to another person, and on his receptivity to accepting God's love from another person. This requires much more from missionaries than simply answering questions or putting up new buildings, however necessary those answers or buildings may be. The effectiveness of this sacrament depends on the transparency of Christ's presence and love in the individual Christian and in his or her community.

Looking at the witness of the lives of the four assassinated White Fathers, I am struck by how closely they lived out the vision of their founder, Cardinal Lavigerie. They were all deeply committed to absorbing the culture and language of Kabylia; they were all involved in promoting the human and spiritual development of the people among whom they lived; and they were all men of prayer and community life. The four thousand people who attended their funeral showed how much they had valued their presence. Perhaps the greatest tribute paid to the White Fathers came from the words of the Muslim referred to earlier, who as a young man had been filled with hatred on his release from a detention camp: "Fr. Jean did not make me a Christian but he led me to God."

On the tenth anniversary of their assassination, a plaque was unveiled at the White Fathers' House in Tizi-Ouzou:

In this place, on December 27, 1994, White Fathers Christian Chessel, Jean Chevillard, Charles Deckers, Alain Dieulangard gave their lives out of love and fidelity.

Msgr. Tessier and the Four Assassinated White Fathers

I asked Msgr. Tessier if he knew the four White Fathers well.

I knew each one of them. Fr. Deckers was based in Algiers and so I used to see him quite often. He had also worked at the Glycines library; he was the chaplain to the Poor Clares; he taught Latin at the university. A while before that I had spoken to him about his teaching at the university, because foreigners were being specially targeted. I asked him if he thought that he should stop giving his classes. He replied, "No. If we stop working and meeting people then there's no reason for us to be in the country." He was very generous. He helped a lot of people.

I used to go to see the three Tizi-Ouzou Fathers fairly regularly at Tizi-Ouzou because this was also the time when the Algerian Catholic community was growing there. And Fr. Dieulangard was looking after them. And then there was also Fr. Christian Chessel, who was younger and whom I wished to accompany more as he was starting his mission in this new environment. I happened to be in Rome when he made his missionary vow as a White Father—that is, his definitive commitment as a White Father—on November 26, 1991. Fr. Dieulangard had been for a long time in charge of the White Father centers for professional training. After that he busied himself with seeking compensation for these centers after their nationalization. We often met to discuss these matters. Then he founded a social services secretariat at Tizi-Ouzou and once again we often met to talk about how it could best meet its objectives.

Fr. Deckers had set out from here, the Diocesan House, at nine o'clock in the morning. I came across him before he left. He was with an Algerian Christian who is still here. I was back here at the Diocesan House for lunch when they were killed at 11:45 a.m. The French Embassy telephoned us to say that three French priests had been assassinated and that, as far as they could make out, a Belgian priest had also been killed. So I knew well that it was Fr. Deckers. Their burial was very moving because the people of Tizi-Ouzou really protested and condemned these assassinations. At the funeral almost all the shops were closed; everyone went to the cemetery. The White Fathers and Sisters had a big presence in Kabylia and consequently we were truly surrounded and supported by the people.

THE WHITE FATHER PRESENCE THREATENED

At the same time, the assassinations were an attack on the important presence that the White Fathers and Sisters had in Kabylia. The attack raised the question of the future of our relationship with Kabylia. Twelve days later the White Fathers were attacked at Ghardaïa on January 8, 1994. Only this time, by the grace of God, they escaped unharmed, jumping into the neighboring garden before the attackers managed to break down the door. Fr. Bernard Lefebvre fractured his leg in several places during the escape. This second attack worried us greatly as we were afraid that it might be part of a concerted attempt to eliminate all the

White Father communities. If the attack against the White Fathers at Ghardaïa had been successful, I think the White Fathers would have been obliged to withdraw their members from Algeria. And then the White Sisters would have followed suit. I think it would have been a free for all. Although the religious brothers and sisters wanted to stay on here, their Congregations were worried as they were under pressure from their families. It wasn't enough that the religious themselves were willing to stay; it was also necessary that their families accept this choice. When families began to put on pressure, saying that to stay on in Algeria was unreasonable and that they would hold their superiors responsible for what might happen, it became difficult for the General Councils to justify allowing the religious to stay. I think the fact that the Ghardaïa Fathers were able to escape harm on January 8 was very important for the future of our Algerian Church, which would otherwise have experienced a dramatic fall in numbers.

CHAPTER SEVEN

A Monastery Set on a Mountainside

The Dialogue of Daily Life

I HAD BEEN THINKING FOR a long time about visiting Algeria; I had even dreamed on a few occasions that I was asking directions in the train station at Algiers! However, I could find no signs in 2003 that would encourage me to visit the country, and the one person whom I consulted in Algeria was unenthusiastic. So, looking for guidance, I said a little prayer, "Lord, show me what I should do!" Two days later, to my amazement, I received a letter from the superior of the monastery at Midelt in Morocco. Fr. Jean-Pierre, the younger, was inviting me to come and visit their monastery, where the survivors of Tibhirine had regrouped. I had completely forgotten about the letter that I had sent to Jean-Pierre six months earlier with an article in English about Fr. Christophe of Tibhirine. I needed no more encouragement. This was the sign for which I had been waiting. So the following year, on July 7, 2004, after an eight-hour delay, I eventually took off from Heathrow airport for Morocco.

The two surviving brothers from the Tibhirine massacre, Jean-Pierre and Amédée, were most welcoming and were very willing to talk about their experience in the years leading up to the kidnapping. What struck me most was how seriously the community of five at Midelt took their life of communal prayer. Office started each morning at 4:00 a.m. with Vigils and ended with Compline at 8:30 p.m. As only two members of the five-man community were under eighty years of age, attending office seven times a day and singing most of it with such a small choir was no mean feat. This indeed was their primary work and witness as monks, and they gave themselves wholeheartedly to it.

The other aspect of their life that immediately struck me was the closeness of their relationship with the local people. The Berbers are renowned for their open-mindedness and their welcome to the monks had been very warm. When the older Jean-Pierre celebrated his golden jubilee as a priest some years ago, more than fifty locals had attended the reception, including three imams. And the few local people who were employed by the monks had a closeness to them that one would expect from blood relations. The charism of Tibhirine had indeed survived its transplantation in tragic circumstances into a new environment. What was the charism of Tibhirine, and why does its story still inspire the Algerian Church and those all over the globe who wish to draw close to their Muslim neighbors?

A Precarious Existence

At the time of writing this chapter, December 2006, the monastery of Notre-Dame de l'Atlas is down to four members, three of whom are over the age of eighty. Such a precarious existence is nothing new to the monks of Tibhirine. In the early 1960s, the monastery was in a similar position and its closure was announced in Rome in November 1963 by Dom Gabriel Sortais, the Abbot General of the Trappists.[1] Cardinal Duval, who was attending the Second Vatican Council at the time, was aghast. He realized that the monastery was vital to the survival of the Christian community, which at that time was hemorrhaging to death, on account of the departure of the European settlers following independence in 1962. Dom Sortais was, however, to die of a heart attack the following day and his decree suppressing the monastery was never implemented. Shortly afterward Cardinal Duval, speaking to the newly appointed Abbot of Aiguebelle, the French Abbey on which Tibhirine depended, commented, "Nine hundred thousand Christians who suddenly disappear is an apocalypse for the Church. If Tibhirine remains, the Church is saved."[2]

Cardinal Duval knew that the Christian Church in Algeria would lose heart without the inspiration that a contemplative community like Tibhirine provided, a community whose raison d'être was not apostolic work—practical, concrete engagement in order to spread the Gospel—but prayer and community life. Not only is a monastic community essential for the well-being of the Christian Church, but it is also a way of life that Muslims instinctively understand and respect. While doing his national service, Fr. Christian was struck deeply by the comment of his friend, Mohammed, who one day said to him, "Christians don't know how to pray."[3] The monastic life, with its emphasis on the Opus Dei, "the work of God," as St. Benedict calls the times of community prayer, is a witness easily understood by Islam, a religion that stresses the transcendence of God and our duty of worshipping him. In the faithfulness of the Tibhirine monks to worship, their neighbors could recognize a strong link with their own communal practice of praying five times a day.

Mohammed, a young Muslim man who had accompanied Christophe on a visit to some of the French monasteries of the order, was heard to say, referring to the Cistercian monks whom he had met, "You know, in France, I discovered some true Muslims."[4] Another Muslim who had visited Aiguebelle showed how he had grasped the essentials of monastic life when he commented that what was vital to monastic life was not making money but the quality of the relationships between the brothers and with God. He added: "For me a monastery must not try to produce more but to pray more and to spend more time with God. Without that, what's the point of a monastery? If one is searching for God, nothing else matters: an onion, a piece of bread is all one needs."[5] The witness of a Christian monastery has an impact not only on the Christian community but also on the Muslims who live nearby.

The Origins of Notre-Dame de l'Atlas

The Trappist presence in Algeria goes back to August 20, 1843, the feast of St. Bernard, when twelve monks from the French monastery of Aiguebelle made a foundation at Staouëli, seventeen kilometers west of Algiers. They had gone there in answer to a request by the French colonial administration, who thought the country would benefit from the Trappist gift for agriculture and that the indigenous Muslim population would be impressed by men of prayer.[6] On July 11, 1846—the feast of St. Benedict—Staouëli was raised to the status of an abbey. However, the life of the monastery came to an abrupt end in 1904, when the Abbot, worried about the anticlerical laws of 1901 in France and a lack of local recruitment, decided to sell the monastery and move to Italy.

The Cistercians returned to Algeria in 1934. The French monastery, Notre Dame des Dombes, had founded a monastery in Slovenia in 1881 to avoid anti-clerical laws in France. The new foundation, Notre-Dame de la Delivérance, prospered. However, in the 1930s the then Abbot, Dom Placide, worried by the insecure political situation, decided to seek out a place of refuge in case flight from Slovenia should become necessary. His searching led him to Algeria in the spring of 1933. An advance party of monks set out for Algeria on March 7, 1934, and arrived in Algiers on March 20, whereupon they proceeded immediately to the Basilica of Notre-Dame d'Afrique to celebrate a mass of thanksgiving. In 1938 the Abbot of Notre-Dame de la Delivérance in Slovenia, judging that the political threat had passed, handed over responsibility for the Algerian foundation to the Abbot of Aiguebelle, the Abbey which had founded the first Algerian monastery at Staouëli. The new foundation, Notre-Dame de l'Atlas, already in the Médéa region, moved to Tibhirine in 1938. In 1947, when it was raised to the status of an Abbey, the monastery numbered twenty-eight monks and was at that time the only Cistercian monastery in the whole of Africa.

As a result of the war of independence, fought from 1954 to 1962, and a lack of local recruitment, the Abbey fell on hard times, which led to its proposed suppression by Dom Gabriel Sortais in 1963. With the backing of the new Abbot General, Dom Ignace Gillet, former Abbot of Aiguebelle, the monastery continued with a new community of fourteen monks. This included the four remaining monks, four monks from Aiguebelle, four from Timadeuc, and two from Cîteaux, one of whom was the new superior, Fr. Etienne Desroches. The community handed over most of its land to the newly independent state and retained just twelve hectares for its own use. In 1976 the monastery was once again threatened with closure by the local authorities and was only saved yet again by the intervention of Cardinal Duval. A new and decisive chapter in the unstable history of Tibhirine opened with the election of Fr. Christian as Prior in 1984.

The Challenge of Perseverance

With the disappearance of the European population after independence, the hope of recruiting local vocations no longer existed. Tibhirine depended for its survival on the recruitment of vocations from existing Cistercian monasteries in France. Given its geographical location, its existence was destined to be precarious. A monastery normally recruits monks to the novitiate from its home country and trains them in the customs of the house and its spiritual traditions. Each monastery, even though it belongs to the same order, in this case the Order of the Cistercians of the Strict Observance (OCSO), more commonly known as the Trappists, will have a "personality" somewhat different from the other houses of the order. Tibhirine had the challenge, under the leadership of Fr. Christian, of blending together monks from four different houses: Bellefontaine, Aiguebelle, Tamié, and Timadeuc. And to complicate matters, Frs. Jean-Pierre, Bruno, Christian, and Célestin had all been ordained priests before entering their respective novitiates and becoming monks. A priest is used to exercising authority and leading an independent lifestyle and may find it more challenging to settle down to a life of obedience in the service of the community. Recognizing this, St. Benedict in his Rule is wary about admitting priests, saying, "If any ordained priest asks to be received into the monastery, do not agree too quickly" (RB 60:1).[7]

Living the monastic life, contrary to the popular, romantic image, is never easy. This shouldn't come as a surprise to anyone who has studied the lives of the saints. The Christian life, although joyful, invariably has its share of difficulties. These trials and struggles, which are part of Christian discipleship, allow the Holy Spirit to purify us and draw us closer to him. For some monks, obedience to superiors and to their fellow monks will be a source of difficulty and most, at some time or other, will find perseverance a challenge— doing the same thing day in day out, even something as wonderful as praising God! In the case of Tibhirine, this challenge was complicated by the isolated geographical setting of the monastery, the size of the community, and the lack of a local Christian community.

In a large community it is easier to escape from those brethren whom one finds difficult and annoying, those with whom one has little natural affinity. In a small community, such as Tibhirine, these escape routes are cut off. Moreover, in a small, poor monastery in a developing country, each monk would be expected to fulfill many roles to keep the monastery functioning. So the same person may have to end up leading the singing week in week out, quite an exhausting task in itself. In addition to seeing countless patients each day in the dispensary, Br. Luc, an eighty-two-year-old medical doctor, also had to help some of the time as monastery cook, rising at 2:00 a.m. to prepare the meals for the day ahead—a task a twenty-year-old would flinch at. A further source of tension was the commitment of their prior, Fr. Christian, to inculturation and dialogue with Islam, an approach that was understood differently by various members of the community. Some brothers, such as Jean-Pierre and Amédée, put the stress on living alongside their Muslim neighbors, whereas Fr. Christian saw the need for a more intellectual and scholarly approach. Living the monastic life at Tibhirine demanded courage and perseverance.

A Praying Community

A person admirably equipped to see the challenge of life at Tibhirine was Br. Philippe Hémon, a monk of Tamié and a friend of Fr. Christophe, who visited regularly to help the community with the renewal of its office. The thing that struck him most on his first visit to Tibhirine in December 1989 was the precariousness of life there. The monks were foreigners belonging to a tiny religious minority in a politically and economically unstable country, and to boot, members of probably the poorest monastery of the Order.[8] Fr. Philippe's first thought was to simplify the office as much as possible in order to lessen the tension and struggle required to keep up a high standard of music with such few resources. However, he quickly realized that he was misguided. The office was the center of their monastic life and the source of their nourishment. It was the reason for their presence in Algeria—to be a praying community alongside a praying people. His task, he realized, was to embellish and make more beautiful their life of prayer, not to impoverish it.

This indeed was what also surprised me on visiting the survivors at Midelt in Morocco. Their main work was the Opus Dei, "the work of God," into which they poured the best part of

their energies. Here indeed lies one of the secrets of the perseverance of the monks at Tibhirine and of their reaching out to their
Muslim neighbors. They had remained faithful to the key intuition
of St. Benedict in his Rule when he stated succinctly, "Indeed,
nothing is to be preferred to the Work of God" (RB 43:3).

That an isolated monastery of just eight monks in a completely Muslim environment could produce individuals of such
human and spiritual depth as Fathers Christian, Christophe, and
Br. Luc is remarkable. However, a monastery never focuses exclusively on the individual. Rather, St. Benedict's vision in his Rule for
monks is that of a community where the talents of each are put at
the service of all. In our individualistic age, such a project may
sound detrimental to the well-being of the individual monk.
However, as St. Benedict well understood, we only flourish as individuals if we have the support and challenge of a community. Such
a setting provides the indispensable environment for learning how
to love, "a school for the Lord's service" (Prol. 45).

Although the community was few in number it was rich in
talents. Fr. Christian was a man of considerable learning as his
almost daily conferences in the community reveal,[9] a man of eru-
dition with a scholarly knowledge of Islam. The novice master, Fr.
Christophe, was also sub prior, in charge of the liturgy and of the
garden that he ran as a cooperative venture with a number of the
villagers. He was also a talented poet. Br. Paul was what every
household treasures, a plumber by trade and a talented handyman.
Given the isolation of Tibhirine and the rundown nature of its
buildings, these gifts were invaluable. Br. Paul also served as Guest
master. Br. Luc, a skilled medical doctor who had chosen to remain
as a lay brother, looked after the medical needs of the villagers and
also doubled, when needed, as the community cook. Br. Michel
was a self-effacing man who worked in the kitchen and at other
practical jobs around the monastery. Before entering monastic life,
Fr. Célestin had worked with those on the margins of society. At
Tibhirine his musical gifts as organist and cantor were put at the

service of the community. Fr. Bruno was prior of the monastery's annex in Morocco. Fr. Jean-Pierre did the community's shopping in nearby Médéa, while Fr. Amédée maintained a special relationship with the villagers. Each of the brothers contributed his gifts and talents for the well-being of all.

The Dialogue of Daily Life

The life of the Tibhirine community was nourished by its ceaseless round of communal prayer in church, by individually pondering the scriptures, and by its community life of mutual service. However, the life of a monastery always has an impact on the surrounding countryside as local people are drawn to it either by its life of prayer, its employment opportunities, or both. What was unusual about Tibhirine was that after Algerian independence in 1962, there was only a skeletal Christian community left to support the monastery, and with the outbreak of the civil war in 1992, no Christian community whatsoever remained in the Médéa region. Once the years of violence had erupted, the local parish priest of nearby Médéa, Gilles Nicolas, found himself with no parishioners except the monks!

However, the monks of Tibhirine succeeded in developing a strong relationship with the local community. Undoubtedly this relationship had much to do with the presence of Br. Luc, a medical doctor, who had served the local village and surrounding countryside in this capacity for more or less half a century. The monastery had also for a long period run a primary school for the village, and in the more recent past the monks had set up, under the direction of Fr. Christophe, the cooperative gardening project with the villagers. Even in a Christian setting, the cooperative project and monk doctor would have been highly unusual. In addition, on account of the presence of the monks, the village of Tibhirine had been spared the prevailing violence and terrorist activity that the other villages in the area had experienced. Since the start of the civil war in 1992, the relationship between the monastery and its Muslim neighbors had grown closer than ever. This relationship was a powerful example of the Christian-Muslim dialogue of daily life.

And, of course, in many ways monks are the ideal partners for such a dialogue. Benedictine monasticism, with its emphasis in the Rule of Benedict on obedience to God's will and on human insignificance before God, or humility, resonates strongly with the teaching of the Qur'an. Fr. Christian remarked that the villagers had never heard of Cistercians, Trappists, or even monks. The villagers had no need of such esoteric labels but were quite clear about the identity of the brothers. They were simply *roumis,* that is, Christians. The *roumis* in their case, according to Fr. Christian, would be understood in terms of the villagers' own religious practice as a person who "prays, believes in God, fasts and gives to the poor…he is almost like one of us!"[10]

An Awareness of God's Presence

A monk is required by the Rule of St. Benedict to put the praise of God first and at the center of his life. The observant monk and the observant Muslim both try throughout the day to recall God's presence in their lives and to center their lives on it. St. Benedict's stress on the "fear of the Lord," a reverential awareness of God's presence in our daily life at all times and in all places, is similar to that found in Islam. In his book *Understanding Islam,* C.T. R. Hewer states that the ultimate aim of the five pillars of Islam "is to train those who practice them, so that they will be ever-mindful of living a godly life. These practices are a training program to build *taqwa,* God-consciousness …"[11] And the Jesuit Fr. Henri Sanson, who spent most of his life in Algeria, wrote: "In Islam, the feeling of God's presence is very strong almost overwhelming. The Muslim leads his life under the constant gaze of God, awaiting the Day of Judgment. He is given over to his omnipresence."[12]

As the muezzin called the villagers to prayer in the prayer room lent to them by the monks and as the last functioning Church bell in Algeria summoned the monks to office, the people of both faiths knew that they were close, perhaps even closer than many realized, as they sought to put God at the center of their lives. Fr. Christian told the story of a young Muslim friend who asked him to teach him how to pray. One day this young man remarked, "It's been a long time since we've dug our well." Christian replied in a teasing manner, "And at the bottom of our well, what will we find? Muslim water or Christian water?" Puzzled, his friend replied, "Are you still asking yourself that question? You know what one finds at the bottom of that well—it's God's water."[13] Prayer and work, *ora et labora,* the well-known Benedictine motto, aptly sums up the dialogue of life that the monks took part in with their Muslim neighbors.

Finding God in All Things

Working alongside the villagers and sharing the daily threat of violence deepened the friendship between the villagers and the monks. With the almost total disappearance of Christian visitors to the Guesthouse in the 1990s, the monks were thrown back on their own company and that of the villagers. Life took on a new intensity for all of them as the possibility of a violent death came ever closer. When suffering and fear enter our lives we have to try to make sense of them, to give them meaning. Otherwise we will end up paralyzed with fear and filled with resentment. The challenge to the Christian is somehow to find God in the fear and in the suffering and so to make them bear fruit. The monastic practice of *lectio divina,* the prayerful pondering of Scripture, allowing God's Word to speak to our personal experience, is a powerful aid to conversion and to overcoming fear and despair. Reading the letters, journals, and homilies of the monks from this period, I am struck by how real God's presence was to them, and how it helped them to accept whatever suffering might come their way for the sake of the Kingdom. As Br. Paul so poignantly expressed it, "The Spirit is at work, he is working in the depths of the hearts of people."[14]

Mary's *Magnificat* is a marvelous example of the fruits of *lectio,* the ability to read God's hand at work in the events of one's daily life. Mary recognizes the "great things" that the Lord has done for her and rejoices in his goodness to her. She also recognizes that it is the lowly and humble who have won God's favor. At Tibhirine the monks had also come to see God's love at work in their lives and in the lives of the lowly and humble followers of Islam who lived alongside them. Their practice of *lectio* had undoubtedly helped them to recognize that, in Fr. Christian's words, "The future belongs to God who in any case, wishes to fill us."[15]

On Holy Thursday, March 31, 1994, Fr. Christian gave a moving homily on the martyrdom of charity, the first of four homilies that he was to give on the subject of martyrdom.[16] In it he reflects on the difficulty of living the everyday realities with fidelity and love, the suffering and courage which this demands. Persevering in the little daily acts of self-forgetfulness and love make up the warp and woof of monastic living, as it does of any Christian life. Fr. Christian faces up to the difficulty of this calling and to our weakness in responding to it. "From experience we know that the little things often cost a lot, particularly when we have to go on doing them day after day. It's all right to have to wash the feet of one's brothers on Maundy Thursday…but how about doing it everyday?"[17] However, despite the many difficulties of community life and the added tensions of living under physical threat, God's grace was wonderfully at work among them. Fr. Christian notes in the community's circular letter of April 1995, "Apparently nothing has changed: same places, same people! And yet…while our characters remain the same with their charm and their rough edges, there is among us something resembling a new quality of harmony and mutual acceptance."[18]

Why Did They Stay?

The threat of death became ever more real for the community with the killing of twelve Croatian construction workers, murdered because they were Christians, in December 1993, at Tamesguida, just a few miles distant from Tibhirine. This threat, as well as increasing the stress under which the monks lived, had also the effect of binding them together more closely than ever. When I met Jean Pierre in 2004 in Midelt, he told me that after the invasion of the monastery on Christmas Eve 1993 by some local armed fundamentalists they had all feared for their lives. The Algerian authorities, worried about their security, had encouraged the monks to move to the nearby town of Médéa, where they would have been given protection by the military. The monks refused and the authorities insisted on increased security measures, including the locking of all doors by 5:30 p.m. Jean-Pierre remarked that what seemed like a cloud of fear would settle over the monastery every evening once the doors had been locked. The monks were to live with this cloud of fear for the next two years. News of the assassination of various Christian religious in Algiers, which arrived with monotonous regularity, did nothing to reduce the tension.

In the community circular letter of April 11, 1995, Fr. Christian didn't mince his words. Referring to the brutal massacre of the entire White Father Community at Tizi-Ouzu a few months earlier, he baldly stated: "We knew them well, each one personally. It was an entire community which was thus wiped out. [We had a] brutal sense of only being a 'fish-tank,' a source of easy victims for other reprisals."[19] So why did they stay if their lives were so directly threatened? Would it not have been more prudent for them to have packed up and retired to Morocco or elsewhere to await better days? This indeed was the initial reaction of the monks to the visit on Christmas Eve.

As Msgr. Teissier states, their initial decision to leave was not on account of fear for the safety of their own lives.[20] Rather they were afraid that the demands of the armed group, especially their demands for money, would compromise their Christian witness. However, they changed their minds following the visit of their archbishop, Msgr. Teissier, and their parish priest, Gilles Nicolas. They decided that their place was alongside the suffering people of Tibhirine. It was decided that some of them would provisionally leave Tibhirine for reasons of health or study and that four or five monks would remain. If the armed group were to put them in a compromising position they would have had no option but to leave. The armed group did return to look for medical help. Br. Luc was always willing to give such humanitarian help without asking any questions and the community saw no moral problem with this position. And on only one occasion did the brothers of the mountain threaten the monks' neutrality by using the monastery telephone.

As well as wishing to show solidarity with the villagers, a second reason for staying was the monks' wish to show solidarity with the beleaguered Christian Church in Algeria. Msgr. Teissier points out that all Christians in the country were under threat of death and that some religious communities were in an even more vulnerable position than the monks.[21] In October 1993 the Sisters of Charity received a written threat against their nursery for abandoned babies. The women supervisors and the babies would have their throats cut if the center didn't close within ten days. The twelve Algerian women supervisors and the sisters refused to close the center and give in to this blackmail. If the monks were to leave Tibhirine in the face of a similar threat, would it not be to allow violence and intimidation to have the final word?

Msgr. Teissier was well placed to meditate on this difficult question of prudence versus evangelical solidarity in the face of threats of violence. His own life was constantly under threat and he had to learn to live with this on a daily basis. He goes on to say in the same reflection that we need to respect the sacredness of human life and not risk it for ideological reasons:

> But how can one renounce risking one's life for people with whom one is in solidarity? It is so much in harmony with what we meet in the life of Jesus and with what we celebrate in the Eucharist...
>
> We are all placed in an exceptional situation where it is necessary to run the risk of dying on account of the ties which God has given us with brothers and sisters with whom we have drawn close on account of the Gospel. All our Algerian friends run the same risk. Many other Christians worldwide also live in similar circumstances. What is perhaps special to our case is that our ties of fidelity have been established with Muslims. Now that is precisely the specific vocation of our Algerian Church.[22]

Do We Really Love the Algerian People?

As we all know, the brothers of the mountain did come on the night of March 26, 1996, kidnapped seven of the monks, and fifty-six days later beheaded them. St. Benedict tells us that we must share patiently in the suffering of Christ if we are also to share in his kingdom (Prol. 50). For fifty-six days the monks entered into the tomb with Christ before emerging into the fullness of life in the light of his kingdom. No one knows exactly what happened or precisely who was responsible for the kidnapping claimed by the GIA. The political machinations and conspiracy theories that lie behind these tragic events will probably never be fully uncovered, and a discussion of them lies beyond the scope of this book. However, the impact of the monks' death has not ceased to reverberate and challenge all those who believe in the power of the sword. The monks gave their lives out of love, love for the Algerian people. In the community's circular letter of April 25, 1995, Fr. Christian poses a rhetorical question: "The certainty that God loves the Algerian people and that he has undoubtedly chosen to prove it by giving them our lives. Well, do we really love them? Do we love them enough? The moment of truth for each one and a heavy responsibility in these times when our friends feel so little loved. Slowly, each one is learning to integrate death into this gift and with death all the other conditions of this ministry of living together which demands total gratuitousness."[23]

Christian's question, "Do we love them [the Algerians] enough?" was answered definitively by the sacrifice of their lives. Jesus himself assures us that "no one has greater love than this, to lay down one's life for one's friends" (John 15:13). And the Tibhirine community had had much practice and preparation for this ultimate sacrifice when they shared their daily life with the villagers—working together in the garden, lending them a room for prayer, tending their sick bodies, and sharing their worries and anxieties. Through living "in prayer, silence, and friendship,"[24] side by side with their Muslim brothers and sisters, they had overcome the barriers of hate and mistrust between Christian and Muslim. To paraphrase the preface for martyrs in the Roman lectionary, their death revealed God's power shining through our human weakness.

What of the future of Notre-Dame de l'Atlas at Tibhirine? Will the monks, or another monastic community, return to sing God's praise within its walls? Despite Msgr. Teissier's best efforts, no community has so far been found. On two occasions in 2006 I concelebrated mass in the majestic cathedral of Le Sacré-Coeur in the center of Algiers. On both occasions there were a handful of faithful present, mainly elderly women. And on both occasions they said to me, "We need a contemplative community. Please come and live among us." Meanwhile, the seven monks lie at rest in the lonely graveyard at Tibhirine.[25]

CHAPTER EIGHT

My Life Was Given to God and to This Country

ST. BENEDICT TELLS US TO keep death daily before our eyes in order to fully appreciate the richness of our existence and the eternal value of our actions (RB 4:47). While in theory it is easy to agree with this maxim, in practice most of us can only pay it passing attention. Christian de Chergé had good reason to take this advice to heart. He, like all other foreigners in Algeria, had been put under sentence of death in October 1993 by the GIA. Faced with the real prospect of assassination by the fundamentalists, Christian's life took on a new clarity of purpose and insight, which he shared in his writing and preaching in the final two years of his life. Christian de Chergé knew that he almost certainly didn't have much time left to live and that the wisdom of his decision to stay on in Algeria and face the possibility of execution would be questioned. So he left us his Testament, a summing up of his long spiritual journey and of his love for God and for the Algerian people. In what follows, I recount some of the key spiritual encounters that marked Christian's life in Algeria and that form the backdrop to this remarkable document.

The Written Testament of Fr. Christian de Chergé of Tibhirine

When an À-Dieu is envisaged…
If it should happen one day—and it could be today—that I should be a victim of the terrorism which now seems to want to embrace all foreigners living in Algeria, I would like my community, my Church, my family to remember that my life was GIVEN to God and to this country.

Christian de Chergé, the second of eight children, was born into a faithful Catholic family on January 18, 1937, in Colmar, France. Ordained a priest for the Archdiocese of Paris in 1964, he entered the Trappist monastery of Aiguebelle in 1969. In 1971 he moved to the monastery of Tibhirine in Algeria, where he would be rooted for the rest of his life.

Fr. Christian wrote the first draft of his Testament in Algiers on December 1, 1993, while waiting for the return of Fr. Amédée from France. The armed Islamic group GIA had issued an ultimatum to all foreigners to leave the country by December 1 under pain of death. This was a way of bringing international pressure on the military government as well as expressing a desire to see an end to Western influence in their hoped-for Islamic state. Christian had committed himself to service of the Algerian Church and of the Algerian people. He was unwilling to turn back as it faced its moment of greatest need.

However, there were also deeply personal reasons why he should be willing, if necessary, to lay down his life for his friends. While on national service in Algeria in 1959, during the Algerian war of independence, he had befriended a local policeman, Mohammed, a father of ten and a devout Muslim. One day an attempt was made on Christian's life while in his friend's company. Luckily Mohammed managed to shield him and save his life. The following day, however, his friend was found assassinated by the roadside. This incident left an indelible mark on Christian. He could never forget that an Algerian Muslim friend had sacrificed his life for him. He would write that he looked forward to meeting him in the communion of saints, "this friend who lived even unto death the one commandment."[1]

Christian wished to live out his monastic commitment in Algeria as a sign of his love for the Muslim people and to deepen his understanding and appreciation of Islam, to become a man of prayer alongside a people of prayer. This vocation to a closer union with Islam was confirmed a year before his final vows in an unforgettable experience on the night of Sunday, September 21, 1975, an experience Christian referred to as "A Night of Fire."[2] Christian returned to the chapel after Compline and prostrated himself in prayer between the altar and the tabernacle. Suddenly he became aware of another presence beside the altar, also prostrated in prayer. The man, who was a Muslim guest in the monastery and scarcely known to Christian, began to pray aloud, praising God from the depths of his being. This was followed by a silence, and then the guest turned toward Christian: "Pray for me." Christian began hesitantly to pray: "All powerful and one Lord, Lord who sees us, you who unite everything beneath your gaze, Lord of tenderness and of mercy, God who is totally ours. Teach us to pray together. You who are the only Master of prayer, You who attract first of all those who turn towards You, You, You, You..." Then another voice joined in the prayer as French and Arabic became inextricably united in one whirlwind of praise as they both sought "to penetrate together the Love which says God." It was then Christian's turn to listen as his companion prayed: "I don't ask you for riches; I don't ask you for power or honors...I only ask you for the Love which comes from You, for nothing is loveable outside You, and no one can love without You. I want to love you in everything. Love is the wellspring, the eye of religion. Love is the joyful consolation of faith." They were at this point joined by a third person, in all likelihood the monastic guest master, who had come to look for the Muslim guest. The symphony of prayer was further amplified "in the fusion of these three different expressions of a single and same fidelity, that of the Spirit who is in God, who says God." The prayer, which had started at 8:00 p.m., concluded after 11:00 p.m., and it had all passed by as if it had been a single instant. Christian never again met this "friend of a single night." The following day all he said to Christian was, "Everything is simple when God is in control." This "Night of Fire" confirmed Christian in his monastic vocation to a Muslim people.

Ribat es-Salam,[3] The Bond of Peace, was a Christian group founded in 1979 by Claude Rault, a White Father, which used to meet for two days twice a year at the monastery of Tibhirine. They wished to develop stronger spiritual links with their Muslim neighbors. While shopping in nearby Médéa, one of the Tibhirine monks, Fr. Jean-Pierre, met a Sufi (a follower of a mystical Islamic tradition) who expressed a desire to get to know the monks. Out of this chance encounter a group of Muslim Sufis joined the Ribat for its meetings at Tibhirine. They weren't interested in dogmatic discussions but in journeying together in prayer. The meetings involved an exchange on a theme proposed alternately by each group and on a time of prayer. Christian would write about these encounters: "There is a fraternal listening to Islam that can bring us back to the very heart of the mystery of God, in a humble attachment to a Christ always greater than anything we can say or live about him."[4] Through his membership of The Bond of Peace he had entered into a deep spiritual friendship with the Sufis, a friendship that demanded fidelity especially at this time of upheaval.

> May they accept that the sole Master of all life was no stranger to this brutal departure. May they pray for me: how could I be found worthy of such an offering? May they know how to associate this death with so many others just as violent, left to the indifference of anonymity.
>
> My life has no more value than any other. It has no less value either. In any case, it has not got the innocence of

childhood. I have lived long enough to know that I am an accomplice of the evil which seems, alas, to prevail in the world, and even of that which would blindly strike me.

I would like, when the time comes, to have a moment of lucidity which will allow me to ask pardon of God and of my fellow human beings, while at the same time to pardon with all my heart the person who would strike me down.

Here Christian draws attention to the mindless violence that was plaguing Algerian society in those terrible years of civil war starting in 1992. An estimated one hundred thousand to two hundred thousand Algerians were brutally murdered, among them nineteen priests and religious and about one hundred lay Christians. He has no illusions about the evil that is flourishing in Algerian society or about the evil that, alas, also has a home in his own heart. As a follower of St. Benedict, Christian has the humility, or truthfulness, to acknowledge his own complicity in the evil of society and to know that his life is no more valuable than the lives of those countless anonymous Muslims, equally loved by God, who have died violent deaths. He only wishes to be given at the time of his death the grace to forgive his assassin.

I could never wish for such a death; it is important for me to state this. I don't see how I could in fact rejoice that this people whom I love should be accused indiscriminately of my murder.

It is too high a price to pay for what will perhaps be called the 'grace of martyrdom,' to owe it to an Algerian, whoever he may be, especially if he claims to be acting out of fidelity to what he believes to be Islam.

Christian is absolutely clear that it would be wrong for him to desire or actively seek a martyr's death. He is called to love his enemies, not to put them in the position of becoming murderers. Nor does Christian wish to stain the whole Algerian people with the shame of such a murder. In a final retreat conference given on March 8, just under three weeks before his abduction, Christian quotes from the Christmas Day sermon in T. S. Eliot's *Murder in the Cathedral,* "for the true martyr is he who has become the instrument of God, who has lost his will in the will of God, and who no longer desires anything for himself, not even the glory of martyrdom." Christian, as a follower of Jesus, is called to pray for his enemies and to pardon them. And his prayer, he tells us, is that God will first of all disarm him and his community and then disarm those who are threatening their lives.[5]

> I know the contempt with which Algerians in general have been treated. I know also the caricatures of Islam which a certain type of Islamism encourages. It is too easy to salve one's conscience by identifying this religious way with the fundamentalist beliefs of its extremists.
>
> Algeria and Islam are for me something else; they are a body and soul. I have proclaimed this enough, I think, considering what I have received from them, finding there so often that straight guideline of the Gospel learnt at my mother's knees, my very first Church, as it so happens in Algeria, and already at that time respectful of Muslim believers.

Here again, Fr. Christian expresses his love for, and appreciation of, the Algerian people. As well as the time spent in Algeria between 1959 and 1961 while doing his national service, he had also spent three years as a child in Algiers from 1942 to 1945, when he was greatly impressed by the sight of Muslims at prayer. He was equally impressed by his mother's assurance that Muslims and Christians prayed to the same God. He couldn't help noticing, however, the indifference of the European settlers towards the native population. Although they lived side by side, there was no social contact between them in Algiers. His mother's respect for Muslims and for their religion made a lasting impression on him. The friendships he made as a monk and his study of Islam allowed him to see beyond the caricatures with which we all like to view those with whom we disagree or who are different from us.

> My death will of course prove right those who have dismissed me as naïve or idealistic: 'Let him tell us now what he thinks about it!' But those people must know that at last my most burning curiosity will be satisfied. I'll now be able, should it please God, to immerse my gaze in that of the Father in order to contemplate with him his children of Islam as he sees them, completely illuminated by Christ's glory, fruit of his Passion, filled by the gift of the Spirit whose secret joy it will always be to establish communion and to re-establish likeness, while playing with the differences.
>
> For this life lost, totally mine and totally theirs, I give thanks to God who seems to have willed it entirely for that special JOY, against and in spite of all odds. In this THANK YOU in which all of my life is now said, I include of course you, friends of yesterday and today, and you, O my friends of this place, alongside my mother and my father, my sisters and my brothers and their families, the hundredfold granted as it was promised.
>
> And you also, friend of the last moment, who will not have known what you were doing. Yes, for you also I want to say THANK YOU and this À-DIEU to you in whom God's face can be contemplated. And may we be lucky enough to meet again, happy good thieves, in paradise, should it please God, the Father of both of us. Amen! Inch'Allah!

Christian expressed the essence of the Gospel, namely, love even of our enemies, in his attitude to the Islamic fundamentalist, the "friend of the last moment," who would kill him. When Christian completed his Testament on January 1, 1994, this forgiveness of a future assassin was not a sentimental appraisal of the situation but a stark possibility. With the invasion of the monastery on Christmas Eve 1993 by the armed fundamentalist group, the GIA, death appeared inevitable. The GIA had issued an ultimatum to all foreigners to leave the country by December 1, 1993, or face execution. In addition, twelve Croats had been assassinated at Tamesguida, four kilometers from the monastery, on December 14 because they were foreigners and Christians. The monks had known these immigrant workers because at Christmas they used to attend midnight mass at the monastery. So when Christian asked to speak to the leader of this armed group, Sayah Attia, he knew he was speaking to someone who had already cut the throat of 145 people, a person referred to in the press as "a filthy beast."

Christian, however, held on to the biblical teaching that "in every person there is something of the eternal," that each person shows forth the face of God. He tells us that in this encounter he was not only the guardian of his monastic community but also the guardian of God's image in Sayah Attia.[6] He had to believe that there was good in Attia despite his having murdered 145 people. And Sayah Attia did respond to Christian's respect for him. He did leave the monastery when Christian pointed out that he didn't wish to speak to an armed man in a house dedicated to peace; he did ask to be excused when Christian pointed out to him that they had arrived armed on Christmas Eve just as they were preparing to celebrate the Prince of Peace, and he didn't cut their throats. (Sayah Attia was himself to die shortly afterward from wounds sustained in fighting.) In this encounter Christian had helped Sayah to discover something of his true humanity. Christian wrote, "People say that these are filthy beasts, they aren't humans, one can't have any dealings with them. As for me, I say: if we speak like that we will never have any peace."[7] Christian refused to write people off.

Even in the worst of people there is a glimpse to be caught of the face of God. He entrusted Sayah Attia to God's mercy.

On the night of March 26, 1996, Christian and six of his fellow monks were abducted by a fundamentalist group; they were beheaded fifty-six days later on May 21. When the moment came to say goodbye to this life, Christian wasn't taken by surprise. He had indeed kept "death daily before his eyes." In his homily for the feast of All Saints on November 2, 1995,[8] he had spoken about confronting death in the midst of life, a death defeated by the Spirit murmuring "Come to the Father." Fr. Christian knew that victory which love alone can bring.

CHAPTER NINE

A Crucified Love

The Journal of Fr. Christophe of Tibhirine

THE JOURNAL[1] OF FR. CHRISTOPHE, the youngest member of the Tibhirine community, allows us to share in his day-to-day living of the monastic life. His journal does not give us access to the romantic picture of monastic living that coffee-table books tend to portray. As anyone who has read the Rule of St. Benedict will understand, monks are very ordinary people, albeit living an extraordinary lifestyle. They are people searching for God in the nitty-gritty of a demanding daily routine. Thanks to Christophe's journal, we can walk alongside him in the last three years of his life as he tried to find God's presence in the suffering of a traumatic civil war.

Fr. Christophe was born on October 11, 1950, in Blois, France, the seventh of twelve children.[2] From an early age he felt called to the priesthood and entered the minor seminary at Tour, where he spent seven happy years. At the end of his high school education he abandoned the idea of becoming a priest and instead opted to follow a four-year law course at the university of Tour. While at university he gave up the practice of his faith and was caught up in the student unrest of 1968, which had swept across France and many other countries. His concern for the marginalized led him to become involved in voluntary work for the homeless with l'Abbé Pierre. However, without a relationship with Christ, he found himself unable to love the poor. After several unsuccessful female relationships he was overwhelmed one night in his student room at Tour by an encounter with love; this unexpected *je t'aime,* "I love you," was to remain the unassailable foundation of his Christian, and subsequently monastic, identity from that moment on: "One day I became aware of your "I love you." I have never gotten over it."[3] In this encounter Christophe had discovered the love which he had been unsuccessfully searching for in his social work and romantic liaisons, a love that would draw him to the monastic way of life.

Notre-Dame de l'Atlas, Tibhirine

Christophe now began the long search that would, after many detours, see him put down his monastic roots as a monk of Notre-Dame de l'Atlas at Tibhirine. After his law degree he spent two years of national service as a coopérant, or aid worker, in Algeria. He lived in Hussein-Dey, a working-class suburb of Algiers, and worked in a center for disabled children. While there he got to know the parish priest, Fr. Joseph Carmona, who introduced him to Tibhirine. In November 1974 he entered the abbey of Tamié in France as a postulant with a view to joining Tibhirine on completing his formation. After eighteen months of life at Tamié, Christophe left, earlier than planned, for Tibhirine. However, his first attempt to live the monastic life in Algeria didn't work out. As a small, isolated monastery, Tibhirine was unable to provide him with sufficient emotional and spiritual support. He returned to Tamié, where he made his solemn profession on January 20, 1980. Nonetheless, Christophe's desire to remain close to the poor was answered when his community at Tamié asked him to return to Algeria. Tibhirine was planning to make a foundation at Fès in Morocco and was looking for volunteers to make this possible. So after many false starts, Christophe finally put down permanent roots in Algeria on October 8, 1987.

Selected Journal Entries

August 12, 1993: Apprentice Martyrs
"One Pentecost day I signed the official form with your declaration: "I love you." What's happening here is a hidden story; it's a game of love or nothing at all."

Fr. Christophe, aged 43, started his journal at Tibhirine on August 8, 1993, describing it as a prayer notebook. The style of prayer that is associated with the monastic tradition, *lectio divina,* involves a slow rumination on the words of Scripture and their relationship to life. Christophe's journal is also a form of *lectio divina,* a prayerful reading of God's hand at work in the events of his daily life. This form of writing is particularly suited to Christophe's gifts, which are poetic and artistic rather than scholarly. The journal form allowed him to explore his inner being and his daily relationships, whether they were with his fellow monks, his Muslim neighbors, or God. This approach, which sometimes results in patches of rather opaque prose, nevertheless has the advantage of allowing him and us to follow the unpredictable promptings of the Spirit.

We're not told what inspired him to start keeping this journal. No doubt he felt the need to ponder the extraordinary events of the community's life and of his own as they collectively and individually tried to make sense of the surrounding violence that drew closer to their door with each passing day. It's not often that a Christian Community has several years in which to prepare for an almost inevitable martyrdom. Such was the prospect that faced Christophe and the other monks at Tibhirine as the ugly face of Islamic fundamentalism and civil war engulfed their adopted country, Algeria.

August 22, 1993: Assassinations
"Assassinations in Algiers. After so many others. This notebook cannot remain sheltered from this violence, which pierces me."

This is the first of many references to assassinations in Algiers and in other parts of the country. These killings reflect the reigning political and social instability in the country, a growing wave of violence that threatened to engulf everyone, especially the fragile and tiny Christian minority. Christophe is becoming more and more aware that his baptism means participation in the life of a crucified Love, a life offered for others.

December 29, 1993: A Source of Wonder
"You, you have still got a small door through which you can leave. As for us, [the Muslim villagers] no, there's no way out, no door."

Christophe is the novice master, cantor, choir master, and he is also in charge of the monastery's substantial vegetable and fruit garden. The monks and a small group of their Muslim neighbors jointly run this market gardening enterprise. The work and the profits are shared. This cooperative venture with the villagers is a great source of companionship and spiritual strength for Christophe and the community. A small Christian island in the midst of a sea of Islam, the monks depend on the support and the goodwill of their Muslim neighbors for survival. And likewise the villagers have found moral and material support in the presence of the monks at Tibhirine since 1938. This collaboration has become so close that a large empty room in the monastery has been handed over to the villagers as a temporary prayer room while they await the eventual construction of their own mosque. Monastic office and Muslim worship thrive under the same roof, while in the nearby town of Médéa violence and religious intolerance flourish. For Christophe, his daily encounters with his Muslim co-workers are a never-ending source of wonder. Mohammed remarks to Christophe that the local Muslims, unlike the monks, have no escape route by which to flee the engulfing violence. And Christophe sees in Mohammed a man whose heart has been pierced by a sword, the sword of violence and the suffering which it brings.

December 31, 1993: To Die without Hatred
"Lord, give us the grace to die without hatred in our hearts."

Br. Luc is the oldest member of the community, a medical doctor by profession and a lay brother. He spends up to ten hours a day looking after the sick who come to him in never-ending streams. He asks no questions of his patients and is willing to tend both sides in the civil war, the brothers of the mountain, as the monks call the terrorists, and the brothers of the plain, as they call the government forces. In the midst of so much violence and hatred, Br. Luc can only pray that the monastic community will not betray the one great commandment of love.

January 15, 1994: To Leave or to Stay
"The massacre of the Croats has traumatized us. Our monastic enclosure does not make us insensitive to outside events."

The massacre on December 14 of twelve Croatian construction workers in the nearby village of Tamesguida came as a great shock to the community. These immigrant workers always came to midnight mass at Christmas, and they had been murdered because they were Christians and foreigners, pawns in the fratricidal war now raging around the monastery. On Christmas Eve, one of the GIA (Armed Islamic Group) leaders, Sayah Attia, and five of his armed followers visited the monastery. It appeared that death was imminent—the feared leader of the group, responsible for the deaths of the Croatians, had in all cut the throats of 145 victims. The killing of the Croats and the visit of the GIA to the monastery on Christmas Eve had a traumatic effect on the monks and confronted them with the painful decision of either leaving Tibhirine or risking the same fate as the Croats. For Christophe, the only defense that the enclosure offers is that of a crucified, non-violent Love.

January 28, 1994: No More Strength
"It's no longer the same. Since their visit, I have no strength left."

Inevitably the traumatic events of December have taken their toll. Br. Michel expresses the tension of living in the shadow of death. Passing the mop to Christophe he murmurs that he has reached the end of his endurance. And Christophe, for his part, wonders about his mental equilibrium.

February 12, 1994: Fidelity to a Suffering People
"What a joy to meet Mohammed, Ali, or Moussa. In them, the Mystery can be glimpsed simply, purely. It's a quality of presence: peaceful, gentle, nourishing."

More and more, Christophe wonders what it means to remain in Algeria and risk one's life in solidarity with the suffering people and the tiny Christian community. And the monks search for answers in their experience of praying the office, of *lectio,* of their community life, and in their friendships with their neighbors, the powerless ones of Algerian society. Being a monk at Tibhirine, Christophe reflects, leads to dispossession, to detachment as they contemplate so much surrounding distress. There is also, however, the detachment "which joy brings: strange, wild, free,"[4] the joy of Jesus' presence among them. Christophe is refreshed by the quality of his simple everyday exchanges with those who work in the garden, a contact with people who radiate the presence of God.

June 13, 1994: Turbulence in the Choir
"To listen to you Jesus in this difficult exchange."

Christophe has the highly strung temperament of the musician and poet. He notes that "there is turbulence in the choir." As cantor and choir master, he finds his role burdensome and distressing, especially when he fails to control his exasperation with other members of the community. He is acutely aware that the uncontrollable forces of violence that are tearing the country apart also errupt in miniature in his relationships with his brothers. Living at such close quarters in a small, isolated community surrounded by violence puts an enormous strain on everyone. Christophe prays for the grace to let go of the aggressive and homicidal response and to put on the humility of Christ. In partaking of the Eucharist he remembers that he is drinking "the blood of nonviolence." To drink the blood of the Lamb puts one in the camp of the victims. "Your victory, Jesus, is not easy in me, in us. I am sure, Love: you win."[5]

Throughout his journal Christophe continues relentlessly to acknowledge within himself his aggressive tendencies, his own bush fires of anger and violence. He finds a remedy to this inner turbulence by honestly acknowledging its presence both in his writing and in his talks with Christian, the Prior, and in his willingness to keep on working at those everyday relationships in the community and with his Muslim co-workers in the garden. As a good follower of St. Benedict, he realizes that the bigger victories are won as a result of fidelity to the little events of everyday life, the helping hand, the welcoming smile. Christophe also realizes that these victories can only be won if he penetrates more deeply into the life of Christ, if his Holy Spirit is at work within him. It is only in conformity to the crucified Christ and his Spirit that Christophe believes new life and growth are possible. This desire to conform to Christ through the gift of his Spirit is a recurring theme in his journal.

October 24, 1994: A Eucharistic Offering
"At the door of the church, at the time of the Eucharist

which they truly celebrated, two Spanish sisters were assassinated at Bab-el-Oued."

This short entry records the assassination of two Augustinian sisters, Caridad and Esther, on October 23. They have entered by the narrow door that leads to eternal life. Christophe is aware that he too needs to pass through the same narrow door of death if he's to join Esther and Caridad on the other side.

December 28, 1994: St Thomas Becket
"Our Church is in tears but her mourning is turned into joy."

The assassination of four White Fathers at Tizi-Ouzou the previous day is recorded. The horror of a violent death relentlessly draws closer. Christophe writes that the role of martyr as victim must be chosen freely so that it may be filled with love and forgiveness. The tears of the Church in Algeria turn into joy as they remember their martyrs: Paul-Hélène, Henri, Esther, Caridad, Alain, Jean, Charlie, and Christian Chessel who are alive in the eternal *I am*.

May 29, 1995: The Victory of the Living One
"This will demand of us a concern for truth: no complacency, no complicity with the homicidal lie."

The blood of so many innocent victims has been spilt. It is in the Eucharist, Christophe reflects, that their commitment to life is born—life is celebrated, the victory of the Living One in the face of the killers. Despite all the signs of death, Christophe sees new signs of life in the monastic community. Their watchwords must be vigilance, availability, waiting. In their resistance to evil, they must become a sign of peace and welcome, a place where the prayer of the resurrected Jesus takes place. Violence and bloodshed are all around. Christophe wonders when his hour will come "to be sown."

January 30, 1996: Islam of the People
"And it is God, encountered in his Word sent among us, who tells me to listen: to welcome all of this strange and singular reality."

Unlike Fr. Christian, Christophe has no academic expertise in Islamic studies or in Arabic. He feels called to encounter the profound Islam of the people beyond the defenses of the fundamentalists and of his own reductionist prejudices. He tries to live this calling by being willing to listen to the humble followers of Islam whom he meets daily in the monastery garden. Christophe is following the advice of St. Benedict in his Rule for monks when he tells us to listen "with the ear of your heart." In this path of humble listening prejudices are overcome and the Spirit is able to draw people into his gift of communion.

Just before his first monastic vows in December 1976, Christophe had a decisive encounter near Algiers with a Muslim man to whom he had given a lift. When Christophe introduced himself, the man said he already knew him. He then proceeded to take out a copy of the Bible, saying that John's Gospel was his favorite book because it is always speaking of love. Moreover, "Jesus is love." He concluded by saying, "We have the same faith. You gave me a lift because we recognized each other."[6] Fr. Christian had his "Night of Fire" shortly before his final monastic vows, when he prayed for several hours with an unknown Muslim, and now it was Christophe's turn to rejoice over this strange encounter with an unknown Muslim who had also recognized that they both belonged to the same God of love.

March 19 1996: Will you come to me?
"I will sing of justice and goodness…I will walk in the way of perfection."

The final entry in Christophe's diary is on the feast of St. Joseph. The journal ends: "I was happy to preside at the Eucharist. It was as if the voice of St Joseph was asking me to sing with him and the child [Jesus] Psalm 100: *I will sing of justice and goodness...I will walk in the way of perfection.When will you come to me...I shall walk with a blameless heart.*"

Christophe was a poet, and the following brief poem dated July 25, 1995, his feast day, sums up his life's desire to be fully conformed to his crucified and risen Savior.

> I ask of you today the grace to become a servant
> and to give my life
> here
> as a ransom for peace
> as a ransom for life
>> Jesus draw me
>> into your joy
>> of crucified love.

The Language of Forgiveness

T. S. Eliot tells us in *Murder in the Cathedral* that the martyr serves to lead people back to God. How did the martyrdom of the seven Tibhirine monks accomplish this? The martyred monks of Tibhirine spoke a very powerful message of forgiveness and reconciliation. They understood that there was no other way of breaking the vicious circle of violence and revenge that had cost so many lives in Algeria. On the death of the White Father Christian Chessel, Christophe wrote, "As your friend, I must pray for your assassins."[7] Likewise Prior Christian, writing in his Testament, in anticipation of a violent death, places forgiveness for enemies at the center of his message. He asks that should he become a victim of terrorism, that he might in a final "moment of lucidity...pardon with all my heart the person who would strike me down."The message of the martyrdom of Christophe and his fellow monks of Tibhirine is one of love and forgiveness, especially of one's enemies. Such love and forgiveness are the fruits of the Spirit. Reflecting on the almost total destruction of the Church in Algeria, Br. Paul of Tibhirine wrote in January 1995: "Nevertheless I believe that the Good News is being sown, the seed is germinating…The Spirit is at work; he works in the depths of people's hearts. Let us be available so that he may act in us through prayer and a loving presence to all our brothers."[8]

CHAPTER TEN

Witness to the Resurrection

A Shared Death

PIERRE CLAVERIE, OP, BISHOP OF Oran, was born in Algiers on May 8, 1938. After his formation as a Dominican in France, he returned to his native country as a priest in 1967. As the civil war that began in 1992 raged, death was Pierre's daily companion, and he took every reasonable precaution to avoid the fate of his Christian and Algerian friends who had been murdered in a ruthless and cruel manner. As Bishop of Oran he won the confidence and admiration of countless Algerians, and his fluent Arabic and deep knowledge of the Qur'an had prompted some of them to speak of him as their bishop too.

On Thursday, August 1, 1996, Pierre had reluctantly agreed to go to Algiers to meet the French foreign minister, Hervé de Charette, who was in Algeria offering support to a beleaguered government. That evening Pierre was anxious to return to Oran; he managed to secure a seat on the 9:30 p.m. flight as a result of a cancellation. When his flight landed, he was met at the airport by a twenty-two-year-old Muslim, Mohamed Bouchikhi, who was helping out at the diocesan center for a part of the summer. The time was 10:54 p.m. The police escort had just driven away when Mohamed and Pierre were flung violently into the air by a powerful explosion as they crossed the threshold of the bishop's house. Their blood was mingled in death.

Mohamed had become a friend of the priest in his hometown of Sidi-Bel-Abbès. He knew that he was risking his life by continuing to associate with Christians, but he knowingly put his life on the line for his friends. He had told Pierre before coming to Oran, "I know that I am going to die but I am going to come because I love you."[1] Pierre also was expecting death. He had angrily denounced the cowardly assassination of Br. Henri and Sr. Paul-Hélène, gunned down as they went about their work of helping students in a poor district of Algiers: "That I should be targeted is understandable: as a bishop, I represent, perhaps in the eyes of some, a despised and dangerous institution. I am a leader and I have always defended publicly whatever has appeared to me to be just, true, all that promotes freedom, respect for people, especially the vulnerable and those in a minority. I have worked tirelessly for dialogue and friendship among peoples, cultures and religions. All of that has probably merited for me death and I am willing to run the risk."[2] Pierre and Mohamed both accepted death rather than give in to a culture of hate and distrust. The death of Pierre Claverie, like that of Jesus, wasn't a simple mishap, something peripheral to his life, but was the culmination of a life given to overcoming the forces of evil.

Fidelity to a Relationship with God

Despite the fact that Pierre was a person of tremendous energy who loved traveling around his vast diocese to meet his tiny, scattered, and disparate flock, his first priority in the midst of a whirlwind of activity remained faithfulness to a life of prayer in community. His faithfulness to prayer, personal and communal, is described by his vicar general from 1990, Thierry Becker, who lived with him in the bishop's house. Pierre rose at 6:00 a.m. and was in the chapel by 6:30 a.m. At 7:15 a.m. they both sang Lauds. At midday he returned to the chapel, and at 12:15 p.m. all the diocesan staff and the sisters joined him there for prayer. He was back in the chapel at 6:30 p.m. to prepare for mass and vespers at 6:45 p.m. In this fidelity to prayer, Pierre found the nourishment he needed to remain faithful to his vocation of preaching the Word and of serving others with a listening heart. His immense activity—keeping an open door to all who dropped in to see him, never refusing an invitation to preach or to give a retreat, maintaining a vast network of friends both Christian and Muslim, and writing countless homilies and articles—all of this apostolic life was based on fidelity to his primary relationship with the God of Jesus Christ. His fruitfulness sprang from this relationship. His total dependence on God can be further seen in the simplicity of his lifestyle as bishop. He didn't have a personal bank account or check book. On his death his friends were surprised to see how little he possessed: a small room with nothing on the walls except a crucifix, an icon, and a photo of his parents. His clothing fitted into two small suitcases and he had few personal mementoes—a pectoral cross that he never wore and a dozen photos—that was it. [3]

Recognition of the Other

Complementing his love of God and springing from it was his insistence on the recognition of the other as other, "The emergence of the other, the recognition of the other, the adjustment to the other have become obsessions." [4] This sensitivity to the uniqueness of each individual was the result of the shattering realization in his early twenties that he had totally ignored and failed to recognize the existence and identity of his Arab neighbors. He grew up in a working-class district of Algiers when the country was under French rule. Unlike the French who lived in the countryside or in small towns, he never had had any Arab friends. He wrote as bishop of Oran in 1990, "We weren't racist, just indifferent, ignoring the majority of the inhabitants of this country." As a Catholic, he marveled that his family could have been so indifferent to its Muslim neighbors: "Love one another...Yes. Love the Arabs also. Perhaps I had been told this but the context of my life didn't allow me to hear it. I have experienced great confusion and bitterness. It was possible to consider oneself a Christian and to be one in good faith...and not to hear, not to see beyond one's Christian frontiers, one's cocoon."[5] The struggle against this tendency to ignore and exclude others who were of a different religion and/or culture became an evangelical imperative that inspired his immersion in the surrounding culture and his countless friendships. Through his mastery of Arabic he learned above all "to speak and understand the language of the heart," to discover a friendship that was deeper than any differences. "For I believe that this friendship comes from God and leads to God."[6] In stressing the importance of friendship, Pierre was continuing to proclaim and live the great teaching and example of Cardinal Duval, Archbishop of Algiers from 1954 to 1988.

Dialogue with Islam

Dialogue with Islam can only be based on respect and love for each other. The other person was, for Pierre, not an object to be exploited, dominated, or possessed, but an equal to be respected and loved. It's only on this basis, he believed, that dialogue is possible between Christianity and Islam. In a conference given in Lille in 1992,[7] Pierre outlined four conditions for a fruitful encounter between Islam and Christianity. The starting point is respect for the other person, his conscience, and freedom. Secondly, we must accept that we don't possess all the truth and that we have need of what the other has to give us; the other may possess a part of the truth that we lack. As Christians we believe that in Jesus, God has revealed to us the fullness of the truth about God and man.

However, we humans do not possess this truth in its fullness and only gradually appropriate it over the centuries. "One does not possess God. One does not possess the truth and I need the truth of others."[8] Thirdly, we need to look at our history more objectively to enable us to live the present together. And finally, more frankness and truthfulness are required in dialogue. An unwillingness to face the truth for fear of offending the other has led to much misunderstanding. In an effort to avoid conflict and a confrontation with "the deep differences which characterize our traditions, we remain with half-truths. Each one only reveals what is likely to please or at least to be accepted by the other, and puts aside carefully what might be problematic."[9] Examples of such differences are the Trinitarian nature of Christian monotheism, the understanding of God's omnipotence, and the identity and role of the prophets in the Bible and the Qur'an.[10] This failure to address differences either through ignorance or a desire not to offend has led to disappointing results in many interreligious encounters in Muslim countries. Pierre adds that unless we are willing to recognize truthfully the great chasm that separates Islam from Christianity, "we are not ready to recognize each other, to know each other, to love each other."[11] To be reconcilers we must be willing to bear the pain of facing reality. Only then can dialogue bear fruit.

A Christian Presence in Algeria

Why should the remnant of the Christian Church in Algeria remain in the country? They have practically no conversions and their numbers are tiny. Why risk one's life in such a situation? Is it not foolish and foolhardy to insist on remaining? In a letter to his friends at Christmas 1994, Pierre referred to the answer given by B. Lapize, SJ, to the same question. Their decision to stay with their suffering Algerian friends was similar to accompanying a very sick person: "I continue to be with you now that the party is over; I want to remain in solidarity, I want to be present in your time of suffering. A useless presence, perhaps, but a gift of presence which indeed speaks of real love. Our presence speaks and gives nothing else except a witness of love. And that, for the bearers of the Gospel which we are, is the most precious message which we can transmit."[12] The Christian community in Algeria lost all of its institutional resources and trappings of power with the nationalizations in 1976. Its only strength now lay, for Pierre, in the quality of its relationships with God and with other people. A former *wali* (préfet or administrative governor of a region) of Oran recalled Pierre telling a journalist in 1996 that his assassination would be a big media coup. However, he refused to consider leaving Algeria despite threats to his life, because his departure wouldn't solve any of the problems but would signal clearly a definite acceptance "that it is impossible for people who are different to get along. In Algeria or elsewhere, including Europe."[13] As a witness to God's reconciling love in Jesus Christ, Pierre knew that his vocation was to remain present in the midst of his suffering people, that this place of human conflict and suffering was where Jesus had chosen to hang on the cross. And as a disciple he had no choice but to follow his Master.

The Promise of the Resurrection

When I started to write this chapter, I spontaneously entitled it "Witness to the Resurrection." The resurrection is also a good note on which to end. In his excellent biography, *Pierre Claverie: Un Algérien par Alliance,* Jean-Jacques Pérennès quotes from a letter written at Easter by a twenty-three-year-old Pierre to his parents: "Christ is risen. There's the foundation of our joy and of our faith…To be sure of the power of the love of the Father, that's the Easter message…It is this certainty lived out in all its inexorable logic which has made martyrs and which means that we Christians must bring joy to mankind, no matter what cross we have to carry. All the message of Easter is in these lines: abandonment to the will of the Father who is love." It is this free and unconditional offering of Jesus' life and of ours "which wins for him and for us the resurrection."[14] Pierre gave his life willingly and unconditionally in the service of love. He truly gave witness to the power of the resurrection in his life and in his death.

PART III:

The Future

CHAPTER ELEVEN

Encountering the Other

A Theology of Presence

PERHAPS THE SIMPLEST AND MOST difficult question that
Christians in Algeria have to answer is: Why are you here?
Likewise, each of the nineteen martyrs had to answer for himself
or herself the same question: Why do you run the daily risk of
being assassinated when you could save your life by leaving? What
value does your presence have in a totally Muslim country and culture? If the Holy Spirit can work and is working through Islam,
what is the specific role of the Christian Church in Algeria today?
Under the dynamic leadership of Msgr. Teissier and three other
bishops, the Church is constantly reflecting on the nature of its
presence in an overwhelmingly Muslim country, a society in which
it seeks to be a leaven and sign of fraternal unity.

The Sacrament of Encounter

The North African Episcopate, CERNA, has produced two major
reflections on the future of the Maghrebian churches—Algeria,
Morocco, Tunisia, and Libya—in post-colonial times. The first docu-
ment, published in September, 1979,[1] was called *Chrétiens au
Maghreb—Le Sens de nos Rencontres (Christians in the Maghreb—The
Meaning of our Encounters)*. A quotation on interreligious dialogue by

the Indian bishops still finds echoes in the writing of Msgr. Teissier and other North African bishops: "The Christian discovers himself as a gift from God and a sign of God's love for the world...His life is essentially a gift received to be shared [with his brothers and sisters who share a common humanity] and it blossoms to the extent that he gives it away."[2] This is one of the key insights, now referred as the sacrament of encounter, which underlies much of the thinking of the bishops as they try to understand how a tiny Christian community can manifest Christ's love in an overwhelmingly Muslim culture and environment.

A second seminal insight for the bishops in their relationships with Islam comes from the second Vatican Council document *Gaudium et Spes:* "For by His incarnation the Son of God has united Himself in some fashion with every man."[3] This teaching has been reiterated by Pope John Paul II in *Redemptor Hominis.* Thus, through the incarnation every person, by the very fact of their humanity, enters into a relationship with God through Jesus Christ. The Holy Spirit continues to work through the Church, but the Spirit is also active in the hearts of those outside the visible Church who work for the betterment of the human family. The bishops state: "The reign of God comes more fully through the knowledge of the mystery of Christ; it is already being fulfilled by the inauguration of the values of justice, truth, freedom, peace and love which are the fruits of the Spirit of God in all human relationships, at the heart of every person as within societal relationships themselves."[4]

The bishops find that this understanding of the Spirit's work is found in the Gospels. Jesus' openness to the outcasts of society and to those like the Samaritans and pagans of his time is noted:

> It is particularly interesting to study the attitude of Jesus toward non-Jews from the perspective which concerns us. We discover in fact that people who remain outside the religious history of the chosen people are considered by Jesus to be models of spiritual openness and of trust in God and in his messenger.[5]

The examples they give include that of the Syrophoenician woman, the Roman centurion, and the parable of the Final Judgment (Mark 7:27; Matt 8:10; Matt 25:31–46). Jesus recognizes faith and trust in God both in Jew and non-Jew: "Jesus' relationship to the non-Jew is one of dialogue and gratitude, not that of proselytism or of exclusion." [6]

A Gospel Presence

To help the Algerian Church deepen their process of reflection, in 1993 the Jesuit priest and theologian Christoph Theobald was invited by Msgr. Piroird, Bishop of Constantine and Hippo, to lead a diocesan day of reflection. As a result of this contact, Christoph was to return to visit the Algerian Church on six further occasions, visiting all of the dioceses and helping bishops, priests, religious, and laity to reflect together on the nature of their presence in a Muslim country. His reflections and experiences develop further the insights of the bishops' documents and have since been published in book form, *Présences d'Évangile: Lire les Évangiles et l'Apocalypse en Algérie et ailleurs. (Gospel Presences: Reading the Gospels and the Apocalypse in Algeria and elsewhere).* [7]

Fr. Theobald's first visit to Algeria was to the diocese of Constantine and Hippo. He was struck by the hidden presence of a tiny community whose structures in the diocese had been reduced by 1997 to a retirement home run by the Petites Soeurs des Pauvres (The Little Sisters of the Poor) and a library in the diocesan center. And yet there was a great network of hidden contacts expressing friendship and solidarity not readily observable to the passerby, the Christian community's only wealth being "the Gospel and their countless encounters with the Algerian people." [8] The concept of Church-sacrament as expounded by the Second Vatican Council seemed to him to be the best way of understanding the role of the Church in Algeria. In fact, Pope John Paul II had referred to this when the North African bishops had made their *ad limina* visit in 1996. He remarked over a meal that "basically you are living what the Council says of the Church. She is a sacrament, that is to say a sign, and one doesn't ask of a sign that it be many."[9] The Church is a sacrament, or sign, of Christ's presence today. As the Second Vatican Council puts it: "By her relationship with Christ, the Church is a kind of sacrament or sign of intimate union with God, and of the unity of all mankind. She is also an instrument for the achievement of such union and unity."[10]

And just as the institutional Church tries to reflect Christ's love for the world in all of her life, individual Christians are also channels and recipients of Christ's love in their daily lives. These relationships are what Fr. Theobald and the Church in Algeria have come to call "sacraments of encounter." They are not to be understood as standing in opposition to the traditional seven sacraments through which the Church transmits Christ's power and presence to Church members, but they are rather complementary to them. They are a way in which Christians confer and receive God's love from others of all faiths or even of none. For Fr. Theobald, the treasure of the Algerian Church is its ability to reflect upon and relate its own daily, humdrum experiences, its sacraments of encounter, to the experience of Jesus, especially in his Galilean ministry: "This to-ing and fro-ing between the stories of daily life and the Gospel stories is absolutely essential because it brings forth the spiritual meaning of what you are living; it has the advantage of transforming these situations into the Word or call of God."[11]

Three Levels of Encounter in the Gospels

Many of the people who meet Jesus in the Gospels do not become disciples, but their meeting with him is a turning point in their lives. Fr. Theobald describes the Gospel "as a school of humanity" in which those who meet Jesus become more fully human without necessarily becoming disciples. We meet such people in the story of the woman with the hemorrhage, the Syrophoenician woman, and others. A second category of people are those who become his disciples and base their lives on an interior fidelity to his teaching. A final group is made up of those disciples who become apostles. Their task is to gather together the group of disciples and to make the Gospel "desirable" to others. Fr. Theobald sees these Gospel encounters as hinging around stories of healing, wherein persons become aware of their own uniqueness and individuality and are no longer afraid to be themselves. Many of these people have lived on the margins of society, but Jesus calls them to assume their own unique destiny. "To become unique vis-à-vis the other, is it not strictly speaking to 'become like God himself?'"[12] These healing encounters with Jesus also take place today between Christian and Muslim; these are also sacraments of encounter.

Fr. Theobald writes that these healing encounters occur when people are able to put themselves in the place of others and to see life from their point of view. They do unto others as they would have them do unto them (Matt 7:12). They are Good Samaritans. They are people of integrity whose thoughts, words, and acts are all of a piece. The sacramentality lies in the event of the encounter whereby the "person-sacrament" brings healing to the other through gestures and words that reveal their own uniqueness. And the persons who are a channel of healing in their turn become more aware of their own identity. This sacramentality of everyday life is a gift of the Spirit unfettered by religious or racial boundaries, as Jairus, the Centurion, the woman with the hemorrhage, the Samaritan woman at the well, and many others discover when they meet Jesus. Fr. Theobald sums up neatly his understanding of the sacrament of encounter: "To be the presence of Christ—people in a sacramental relationship—it is finally to release that which is more human, it is to allow the person met on the road to have access to their unique humanity, it is at last to discover—in this admirable exchange—one's own humanity."[13]

The sacrament or the outward sign lies in the relationship established with another person, a relationship that becomes a source of new life for both parties.

In Algeria the vast majority of encounters are at the level of those passersby whom Jesus meets and who don't become his disciples. He enters into a healing relationship with them, helping them to become more themselves, to claim their own humanity and identity. The many in Algeria whose conscience has been stirred by violence and injustice and who are working for the common good—these, says Fr. Theobald, are the people who are called "happy" in the New Testament because they have listened and responded to the voice of the Spirit at work within their hearts: "Each time that conscience and relationships overcome violence, each time that a link is made and strengthened by means of a significant encounter, and that sometimes at the price of someone's life, the Spirit of holiness is at work."[14]

A Healing Encounter

The many stories told by Christians of their encounters with Muslims confirm Fr. Theobald's analysis. Of course, before presenting us with his insights, he had made seven visits to the Church of Algeria and had listened carefully to what the Church there had to tell him. The story that perfectly describes the first stage of Christian/Muslim encounter, the everyday encounter with another, was told in a letter to the White Fathers after the assassination of Jean Chevillard. As described in Chapter 6, the letter writer, a Muslim, had met Jean on being released from a detention camp in 1959. He was full of hate for the colonizers. On meeting Jean, his heart was touched by Jean's goodness and his own hatred began to melt. He writes, "Fr. Jean did not make me a Christian but he led me to God...and I was able to exorcise the evil which possessed me."[15] This is the type of encounter that Jesus has with people in Galilee who do not necessarily become his disciples. Their lives are changed by meeting him and they find a new sense of identity and healing. In meeting Fr. Jean, this young Muslim was restored to himself and his desire for revenge against the colonizers who had trampled on his dignity was gradually overcome. Jean's luminous goodness had healed this man of a cancerous growth that was threatening to kill him spiritually. He had not become a Christian, he had not experienced the sacrament of reconciliation, but he had come closer to God and had grown in his capacity to love himself and to love others. His meeting with Jean Chevillard was what Fr. Theobald calls a "sacrament of encounter."

And, of course, these healing and revelatory encounters are not all one way. The Holy Spirit is also at work in the lives of Muslim people and working through them to bring healing and wholeness to Christians. All of humanity is made in the image and likeness of God, and what this humanity can become has been further revealed to us through the incarnation, God becoming human in Jesus. We are all called to share in this fullness of humanity that Jesus has revealed to us, a fullness that is the work of the Holy Spirit. In encountering Muslims, Christians have found that their own humanity and well-being have been enhanced. They have learned to love in a more profound way; they have discovered God's own life deep within them. Fr. Theobald refers to the story of the Samaritan woman at the well in Chapter 4 of John's Gospel. Jesus tells her that he can give her "the gift of God," living water welling up within her which leads to eternal life. In the sacrament of encounter, Christian and Muslim offer each other just such a gift when they enable each other to make contact with God's living presence within each other.

A Sharing of Hope

In his recent book, *Chrétiens En Algérie: Un Partage D'Espérance (Christians in Algeria: A Sharing of Hope)*,[16] Msgr. Henri Teissier puts flesh and bones, so to speak, on the theology of the sacrament of encounter. He outlines the history of the Christian presence in Algeria and explains why he thinks the Christian Church has a continuing witness to offer in the face of fundamentalism and intolerance. For Archbishop Teissier, the mission of the Christian Church in Algeria is not mainly concerned with maintaining church services or Christian formation; there is, in fact, practically no indigenous Church left to maintain. The key to their presence is the call to draw nearer to their Muslim brothers and sisters in a spirit of service. The Christian mission in Algeria is lived out in weakness. And this, Msgr. Teissier believes, has become a blessing for the Church there. It has allowed them to draw closer to the Algerian people. With the loss of their schools and other institutions in 1976, the religious were free to go and live in small groups in villages and poor areas that had never known a Christian presence. When Christians were numerous at meetings and gatherings, Muslims were hesitant to join them as they felt out of place. This no longer applies. Though few in number, their contacts with the Muslim population are not insignificant.

Archbishop Teissier takes as an example a talk that he was invited to give in the city of Mascara about the relationship between Christians and the Algerian national hero, the Emir Abdelkader, a native of the city. The city contains a total of six Christians, two priests and two sisters working in education, and two European women married to locals. However, the two priests and two sisters are known and esteemed by most of the people. Three hundred people attended his talk. During his three-day visit, Msgr. Teissier met dozens of people, all Muslims, more freely, perhaps, than if he had been on a pastoral visit in a Christian country. Msgr. Teissier wouldn't like us to think that he rejoices in their small numbers. In their weakness, however, they are more conscious that God is calling them to go beyond the boundaries of the Church and to share God's reconciling gift in Jesus Christ with everyone.

Responding to Fundamentalism

How does Msgr. Teissier cope with the intolerance and violence that are so much a part of the Islamic fundamentalist movement in Algeria? The main Christian response to the violence and intimidation has been to live as normal a life as possible, going to work and serving the common good. When the armed groups gave an order in 1995 for all pupils to stop going to what they considered to be religiously unacceptable state schools, seven million nevertheless continued to attend school. And the Christian-run libraries for students continued to function. Out of this witness of fidelity to the demands of everyday life is born hope for the future. When the Cistercian monks were planning to return to their monastery at Tibhirine, the Abbot General said to the local Muslim people that he did not wish to endanger their lives by having the monks return to the village. They replied that their lives were in danger anyway but "that when you are absent we live them without hope. If you return we will live them with hope."[17]

There has not been any formal dialogue between Christians and Muslims in Algeria. The present conflict is one between two opposing political and ideological currents within the Muslim population. Dialogue with Muslims has not come about in a theological context. Experience has shown, says Msgr. Teissier, that such a doctrinal dialogue leads to mutual incomprehension, as discussion gets bogged down in different understandings of prayer, moral and religious life, salvation, history, and so on. A much more fruitful terrain for dialogue has arisen as a result of the recent upheavals in society. The violence, lack of respect for individuals, and the subsequent social impoverishment have troubled the conscience of many people. In this context of moral confusion, Christians and Muslims have begun to discuss the role of religion in society, women's rights, and the recourse to violence. Christians have won a new respect from the Muslim population as a result of their refusal to abandon the Algerian people in the face of violence.

The ensuing dialogue has a spiritual content as people's consciences are informed either by reference to the Gospel or to the Qur'an. What all this involves is, in Msgr. Teissier's words, *un partage d'humanité*, "a sharing of a common humanity." This concept is best explained by a visit that Msgr. Teissier recently received from a Muslim man of humble background. He was upset by a decision taken to move a retired priest who had just spent a year in his town near Algiers. The priest had given French lessons to the young and to the adults and had mixed with the local people. This Muslim man asked tearfully why the priest had to leave. "All we're looking for is a little humanity; we found it with Father."[18]

Working at Relationships

In the current tense political situation, where Muslim and Jew move further apart in the Holy Land and where extremism elsewhere is flourishing in the aftermath of September 11, we may be tempted to despair. Henri Teissier has a simple but difficult message for us. The way to mutual respect and peace requires a commitment to working at relationships. It is in human friendship that prejudice and bitterness are overcome. Dialogue on a personal, everyday level must be persevered with. Msgr. Teissier gives a wonderful example of how this works in practice. Some Berbers in Kabylia have recently converted to Christianity. The penalty for such an act according to the Sharia is death. A Muslim woman journalist of a fundamentalist persuasion interviewed Msgr. Teissier about this issue. While faithfully reporting his remarks, she also published alongside the interview her request that Muslim converts to Christianity should be put to death. Archbishop Teissier phoned the journalist to tell her that this position amounted to a declaration of war on the Christian community. As the following day was National Handicap Day, he invited her to spend the morning with him visiting a center for the handicapped jointly run by

Christians and Muslims. She accepted his invitation and they spent the morning together exploring this common commitment of Muslims and Christians to other people. By the end of the morning they had come closer to each other. They had lived out, to some extent at least, a sacrament of encounter.

CHAPTER TWELVE

What Hope for the Future?

BECAUSE OF THE INTIMATE NATURE of the small Christian Church in his archdiocese, Archbishop Teissier knew each one of the nineteen assassinated priests and religious well and shared in the emotional trauma of their deaths. He writes:

> "I disembarked at the airport of Satolas at the end of December 1994, accompanying the coffin of the youngest of the four White Fathers assassinated at Tizi Ouzou. We were welcomed on landing by the representative of Algerian Air at Lyon, a laywoman of Danish nationality, married to an Algerian, who knew and loved our Algerian Church. On seeing me distraught, she whispered in my ear, unbeknown to the other airport employees, *Sanguis martyrum, semen christianorum* ("The blood of the martyrs is the seed of the Church"). I must admit that I had difficulty in accepting this phrase of Tertullien.[1]

Now, as I write this book in August 2006, just ten years since the last of the nineteen martyrs, Pierre Claverie, met his death in Oran, I wonder: Have these deaths been in vain, or will they produce a rich harvest for the Church in Algeria and for humanity?

Solidarity in a Time of Danger

Fr. Gilles Nicolas, former parish priest of Médéa and teacher of mathematics in the local Lycée, experienced the years of violence from the inside, so to speak. When he was first appointed to the post of parish priest, he had a few parishioners, but with the increase in violence he had ended up on his own, apart from the nearby monks of Tibhirine. The only *roumi* in the town, he was an easy target as his timetable in the school could be easily known. Despite having put his life on the line every day, he doesn't regret the risks he ran. The fact, says Fr. Gilles, of sharing in the tensions and dangers of every-day life now means that the Church is no longer regarded as a colonial remnant but as part of the Algerian landscape. "The fact of having continued to teach in this context [of violence and personal danger] means that when I go back from time to time to Médéa I am one of them and welcomed into many families." And during the troubles Algerians constantly said that they had need of this Christian presence and solidarity. As the sole Christian in Médéa, he writes: "It was obviously Algerian friends and Muslims whom I met everyday, and together we commented on the evolving situation. I shared their values, their joys, and their sorrows. They had the same hope for this country. Christians in Algeria, a sharing of hope, that is truly what we lived."[2]

New Challenges

In January 2000, a document titled *Les Églises du Maghreb en l'An 2000, (The Churches of the Maghreb in the Year 2000)*[3] was published by the North African Bishops, addressing the question of the future of their Church communities. First of all, it summarizes the history of the Church presence in these regions and comments on the post-colonial loss of institutional power:

The Church now experiences a greater precariousness but in the long term this humble and precarious situation brings us closer to the Gospel. For most of us the paths of interreligious dialogue occur as a result of the encounters of daily life.[4]

This document looks at the political and social aspects of the Gulf War, the rise of Islamism, and also the challenge of globalization. Globalization, symbolized by the aerials that pick up satellite television from all around the world, poses the problem of a pluralist society that even an Islamic country like Algeria cannot escape. In these circumstances, the Christian Church can be both a sign and a point of reference:

She is a sign that pluralism is possible in Maghrebian society and that beyond a simple tolerance, a common future is foreseeable. It is thus that she is seen by many. Our very presence is an invitation to society not to be too inward looking. It can even become for some a point of reference. The latter, in their personal searching, have need of someone who will listen attentively to their questioning and also of a word which might echo their inner thoughts.[5]

It is in the context of this rapprochement between the Christian presence and the aspirations and questioning of many Muslims troubled by the years of violence that the Church can become a leaven in Algerian society. Msgr. Teissier poses the challenge for the Church:

The new times are not concerned solely, however, with the social cost of the Algerian crisis or the consequences of globalization for the economy of the country. These times are marked by a broadening of the questions being posed by those around us. The time of clear-cut certainties, political, ideological or religious is over. Each one, young or old, believer or not, is finding within themselves new questions. Many wish to share these with us although we don't belong to their religious community. Sometimes it is even the difference which we represent, including our religious difference, which attracts our partners and encourages them to put before us questions of conscience with a frankness unknown to us in the past. These developments put our relationships with our Muslim partners in a new context. Are we ready to listen? Have we got a sufficient knowledge of the life of the individuals, of their traditions, their language, their religion, their history so that our replies to the questions which they put to us might be helpful?[6]

The Evangelicals in Kabylia

A further issue that faces the Catholic Church in Algeria is the recent success of various evangelical sects, especially in Kabylia. The estimate of the number of converts in Kabylia varies wildly, with some newspapers reporting that more than half of the population has now become Christian. In reality there are approximately fifteen evangelical churches with anything from three thousand to ten thousand Christian converts. When the Catholics and evangelicals came together a few years ago for a service at Christmas in Tizi-Ouzou, there were about seven hundred people present. There are many reasons put forward for this wave of conversions, which have been mainly, though not exclusively, centered in Kabylia: the refusal of the Kabyles to identify with the Arab-Islamic culture of the country; the strong presence in the past of the White Fathers and Sisters and of Protestant missionaries; the broadcasting of Christian radio and television programs in Arabic and Berber; the dissemination of Christian texts in the local language; the moral confusion experienced in the face of the Islamic violence, and so on. However, two principal causes can be identified for the recent conversions starting in the 1990s, namely, the moral crisis in Algerian society provoked by the traumatic civil war and the refusal of the Berbers to identify with the dominant Arab culture. The evangelicals are eager to make converts and are not sensitive to the social and political consequences of their proselytism. Their theology is very much a pre-Vatican II position of seeking to baptize Muslims at all costs, without sufficient respect for their conscientious beliefs. Establishing a moderating influence on these evangelical groups is one of many new challenges facing the Church.

In a paper given on January 28, 2005, at a diocesan day of reflection, Msgr. Teissier discussed the challenges that these new Christian communities pose for the Catholic Church in Algeria.[7] He points out that this phenomenon of Christian communities being formed out of Muslim families has never before been known since the origins of Islam, hence the uncertainty as to how the Christian Church should react. The theology of these groups concerning salvation and the sacramental life is not shared by the Catholic Church. However, Msgr. Teissier goes on to say that it would be a source of scandal if the Muslim community saw the evangelicals and the Catholics as competitors, or even as enemies. While making clear to Algerian society that the Catholic Church is not behind the establishment of these groups, nevertheless it must also be made clear that the Church respects their right to exist provided they do not exert pressure on people to convert. The answer once again is to be found in encounter. Catholics must seek out occasions to meet and to get to know the evangelicals so that the theological divides can be put to one side: "We must go beyond the barriers established by theology, by international structures or by history by creating, through human contacts, relations of trust and mutual respect."[8] Ironically, the lessons learned in establishing trust and mutual esteem with Islam are now also being applied in establishing good relationships with the new communities of evangelical converts from Islam.

The New Law on Christian Worship

Alarmed by the exaggerated reports in the media of conversions in Kabylia, the government responded by introducing a new law promulgated on February 28, 2006, regulating the conditions and the rules for the practice of non-Muslim worship. This restrictive law has also been seen by some as an attempt by President Bouteflika to appease the Islamists. Worship may now take place only in specially designated buildings, open to the public and identifiable as churches. This, in effect, is an effort to put an end to the proliferation of "house churches" in Kabylia. Religious services may be organized only by officially recognized bodies and buildings will be licensed by a commission appointed by the ministry for religious affairs. Anyone convicted of encouraging a Muslim to convert, or who uses any audiovisual or other means to achieve that end, will be subject to a three- to five-year prison sentence and a fine of five thousand to ten thousand euros.

The introduction of these draconian penalties has come as a shock to the Christian community. Furthermore, the interpretation of these new laws is open to abuse. Although the Constitution allows freedom of conscience and religious practice, the new laws give scope for the restriction of these rights. The Methodist pastor, Hans Hauzenberger, is quoted as saying: "If I am talking over a cup of coffee with a Muslim neighbor and I speak about Jesus, would that be considered an act of proselytizing? Would I fall foul of this new law?"[9] Much also depends on the composition of the commission that will regulate the granting of licenses to church buildings. Will the fifteen or so evangelical churches in Kabylia be recognized? Both Msgr. Teissier and the Bishop of Laghouat, Msgr. Claude Rault, have expressed regret at the severity of the legal penalties. Msgr. Rault comments in his diocesan bulletin: "We continue to value respect for conscience, without for that matter trying to escape, through fidelity to our own, from those who ask us to give an account of our Hope, with the respect and courtesy natural to every Christian."[10]

An evangelical Christian from Kabylia told me: "As for the new law on religious worship, for the moment it's not causing us any problems since the churches here are house churches, hidden churches. As a result they are difficult to get to know and to penetrate if one doesn't know someone who is a member. As well, we avoid preaching in public and showing our faith in public, for, to tell the truth, we are a little afraid. However, thanks be to God, for the moment we don't have any problems." One hopes that the situation as described above by this evangelical will continue.

Algerian Christians

The Inter-Diocesan Assembly of the four dioceses of the Algerian Church held its first-ever general assembly in September 2004.[11] According to the Assembly, one of the major challenges facing the Church is to encourage Algerian Christians to take a more active role in the public life of the Church. The number of native Christians is at most a few hundred. After the War of Independence and the recent civil war, most of the native Catholics, predominantly from Kabylia, emigrated to France, where they now number about eight thousand. The situation of those who have remained isn't easy. Most Algerians regard someone who becomes a Christian as not only an apostate—and the penalty in the Qur'an for apostasy is death—but as someone who has also betrayed his identity as an Algerian. For these reasons most of the Algerian Catholics are forced to conceal their religious identity and are consequently unable to play a public role in the life of the Church. Finding new ways of listening to the experience of these native Christians and of integrating them more fully into the life of the Church is vital for the future of the Catholic presence in Algeria. These native Catholics are growing in number in the aftermath of globalization and the recent cultural upheavals brought about by the civil war. The Inter-Diocesan Assembly recognized that in order for the Church to become truly inculturated into the life of the country, she will need to encourage these new native members to develop "a manner of praying, community living, and witness that are adapted to the country and its culture."[12]

A Day of Great Joy

The future of the Church in Algeria lies ultimately in the hands of God. Humanly speaking, despite the apprehension aroused by the new laws on religious worship and proselytism, there are encouraging signs. Perhaps one of the most encouraging of these has been the recent ordination of Jordi Llambrich by Msgr. Teissier on June 24, 2005, in the Sacré-Coeur Cathedral, Algiers. Jordi is a Vincentian and this order has been present in Algeria since 1646, with perhaps a break of a few years around 1830. Among his many friends attending the ceremony were Muslims from his parish of Bordj el Kiffan. The diocesan magazine carried an extensive account of the ceremony and the celebrations afterward, the first priestly ordination since that of the martyred Fr. Christophe of Tibhirine in 1990. A small article recounted his welcome home by his parishioners, his Muslim neighbors and friends:

LIKE A MARRIAGE

Thursday evening, the courtyard of the parish house of Bordj el Kiffan filled up with neighbors and friends who had come in family groups to celebrate the ordination of Jordi. Chairs and tables had been installed to share a garnished couscous which the neighbors had spent the whole day preparing, accompanied by lively music. And there was enough for the two hundred guests! Young people from the neighborhood act as volunteers to serve the meal and clear up afterward; there are children everywhere. Then a huge bonfire is lit in the middle of the courtyard and Fr. Christian Mauvais explains to everyone the meaning of Jordi's ordination; he introduces the confrères who have come from France for the celebration and thanks everyone for having gathered to be with them. Then it was time for everyone to dance, Muslims and Christians. A great and joyful evening shared in peace...To conclude, the superior of the Vincentians said, "For the Vincentians it is important to be on mission in Algeria and seeing all these brotherly encounters, we can say that something durable is being built."[13]

A Force for Renewal and Reconciliation

In April 2005 I visited the places associated with the martyrs and the various libraries and other institutions run by the Church. Everywhere I sensed a spirit of energy, friendship, and optimism. From time to time I was reminded of the difficult conditions under which the Church community functions. Msgr. Teissier is still required to have a police escort, and the security at the airport and on the roads leading in and out of Algiers is tight. My second visit in April 2006 was more fraught. I sensed a certain tension within the Christian community as they wondered how the new law on worship would be implemented. In addition, the release a few weeks previously of hundreds of Islamists from prison meant that people were tense in case violence on a large scale should flare up again. Police escorts for Msgr. Teissier had been increased and people visiting Tibhirine had had their escorts reinstated. The Church, however, has become used to living with uncertainty and the strength of its relationship with the Algerian people is its best guarantee of acceptance now and in the future.

The two aspects of Church life which had most struck me on both visits were, firstly, the easy nature of relationships between Muslims and Christians and, secondly, the dynamism of Church life. Despite being a small and aging community, there were a great number of social projects, from libraries to holiday camps for deprived children; much theological reflection; and many opportunities for Christian formation. Above all, I sensed that the Church wasn't centered on its own internal problems, but rather focused on how it might contribute to the well-being of Algerian society. Msgr. Teissier is optimistic about the future of Christianity in Algeria if Christians remain faithful to their mission to freely love their neighbors. People of goodwill will recognize in this sincere love a gift from God that must be preserved. He is happy to remain in Algeria: "I give my life here and now freely because God has chosen me as a sign and an instrument of his love for the Algerian people and this choice gives me joy."[14]

Living with Difference

The witness of the nineteen martyrs has brought to the attention of the wider Church the life and dynamism of this tiny Christian remnant in an overwhelmingly Muslim country. The Church in Algeria and its nineteen martyrs have absorbed the teaching of Vatican II and its return to gospel values in our relationships with other religions. In the sacrament of encounter, a new realization of what unites Christians and Muslims has been discovered, a realization that through the power of the Spirit at work in our common humanity we can reach out to each other in friendship, service, study, and prayer.

The nineteen martyrs of Algeria have helped to signal the way for the wider Christian Church as she attempts to draw closer to Islam. The Algerian Church has learned to live in weakness. From being the Church of a colonial power, through a series of deaths, she has become a Church of a faithful remnant, powerless and at the service of a Muslim people, whereas the Christian Churches in the West still occupy a position of power and dominance in relation to the Muslim minorities in their midst. The message of the Algerian Church and of her martyrs for us is so simple that we can easily overlook it. We have to learn above all to get to know our Muslim neighbors, to rejoice in our common humanity, to see them as channels of God's love for us. In this way we will learn to live with difference and to be enriched by it. With Fr. Christian of Tibhirine we can learn to contemplate God's face in that of our Muslim brother or sister. The nineteen lives offered out of love for their Muslim neighbors witness to the depth of friendship and love that Christians and Muslims can have for each other. In this love lies a sure hope for the future.

CHAPTER THIRTEEN

God's Gift to Us— An Interview with Msgr. Teissier

Msgr. Teissier: A Man of Great Energy and Devotion[1]

THE PERSON WHO MOST SYMBOLIZES the desire of the Algerian Church to be a force for renewal and reconciliation is Msgr. Teissier. Before visiting Algiers, I had met Père Teissier, as he's usually called by his flock, during a brief visit that he had made to Worth in January 2002. He is a man of great energy, and he is utterly devoted to serving the Church and the Algerian people. He is a humble man who lives in an apartment in the Diocesan House. He eats his meals with the staff and various groups that constantly make use of the building, and he is totally available to his people. For example, he didn't seem to find it unusual that an Algerian Christian should phone him at seven o'clock in the morning to share her delight at having at last found a job.

Msgr. Teissier celebrated the fiftieth anniversary of his priestly ordination on March 23, 2005. The tribute paid to him on this occasion by André Barakat, a Lebanese Christian living in Algeria, struck me as summing up very well the person whom I had come to know. He found Msgr. Teissier's humility and sincerity touching. "You are present to each one of us, knowing each by name and always finding a consoling word, which recalls for me Jesus' words in the Gospel of John, 'I am the good shepherd. I know my own and my own know me' (John 10:14). Your dynamism and attentiveness witness to your faith as do your speech and smile which fill the heart of every person who knows you."[2] André failed, however, to mention another notable quality of Msgr. Teissier, namely, his playful sense of humor. After all, humility and a sense of humor go very much together!

Msgr. Teissier first set foot in Algeria in 1947, and his love of the Algerian people has been at the center of his life ever since. It is this love that has enabled him to understand this country's people in a special way. His ability to relate to everyone he meets is legendary. As one Algerian said to me, "Msgr. Teissier listens to you and gives you the key to find your own solution to the problem that you have brought him." The Church and the people of Algeria have been truly blessed by having such a holy and gifted pastor. In the following interview, which took place in Algiers in 2005, he shares his insights into the meaning of the Christian presence in an overwhelmingly Muslim country.

How do you see the future of the Algerian Church?

It's a Church for the most part made up of foreigners, even if they have taken out Algerian citizenship. But they are foreigners who wish to commit themselves to Algeria and to relationships with Algerians, working in solidarity for the common good in Algeria. We see our relationship with Algerians and our witness within Algerian society as an expression of our Christian fidelity. These relationships establish a very strong bond between our little group and Algerian society. Moreover, almost all of our social services, if not the totality, are at the service of Algerian Muslims. Most of our relationships are with Algerians Muslims. It is this relationship with the Algeria of Algerians which we are trying to make evangelical and which is at the center of our vocation. As our community is very small, we need obviously to take into account the existence of the vast majority of the population, which is made up of Algerian Muslims.

You have a very important role to play, as many commentators say that the twenty-first century will be about the encounter between Islam and Christianity. Is it already happening here?

It is very clear that for us, given that there are thirty million Muslims and a few thousand Christians, that we cannot ignore that society is Algerian. We have to live all the events of the life of the Church from within this Algerian society. Pope John Paul II has just died and, of course, we are concerned like all Catholics about this death. But we are even more concerned about the way in which the Algerians received this death. What message had the Pope given to them? Were they moved by this event and thereby enabled to leave behind the centuries old barriers which have kept Christians and Muslims in opposing camps? Were they able to arrive at a stage where both sides could show esteem and welcome for the Pope's message, the message of the Gospel?

All of that is the fruit of Vatican II?

It's the fruit of Vatican II. Without exaggerating, our little community played a role in this theology of Vatican II. The White Fathers have been in Algeria since 1868 and had already experienced for almost a century a relationship with Muslims. They had been specially founded to become educators, spiritual and human, of a Muslim people in Algeria and in Tunisia. The de Foucauld family developed in a similar vein and thus our Church before Vatican II had lived this experience. Cardinal Duval had also committed himself to the same path. During the war of independence, certain priests of the Mission de France already thought that a Church which is for the people isn't a Church which is just for its own faithful. What we had experienced in this domain was brought to Vatican II by several of those who drew up the text of *Nostra Aetate,* people like Fr. Anawati, Fr. Cuoq, Fr. Lanfry, Louis Gardet. Most definitely the Second Vatican Council had opened this horizon by showing that God was active beyond the boundaries of the Church. *Gaudium et Spes* says, for example, that there is a human vocation that is the common to all, that God individually calls all human beings to fulfill themselves by entering into the movement of fraternal love which Jesus has taught us. God's Spirit is present interiorly not only to Christians but to all people of goodwill. This was the basis of our collaboration with our partners: the conviction that the message which is explicitly expressed in the Gospels, the message of brotherly love, is interiorly suggested by God's Spirit to the conscience of all upright people in the country. And we must come together to obey this call.

The word dialogue *is much used these days. What do you understand this word to mean?*

We prefer the word *encounter* because there is a certain ambiguity in the word *dialogue.* It suggests academic or university discussions, colloquiums, whereas with the word *encounter* one can easily see that it is a question of a relationship between persons, some of whom are Christian and some Muslim. We like to use the expression the "sacrament of encounter" to say that in this encounter God gives us something through each other. We as Christians receive something from our Muslim partners which is a gift of God for us and which comes through them, and we think that they also receive a gift of God which comes through whom we are, our Christian identity, etc. We prefer this expression "sacrament of encounter" to "dialogue" but that doesn't deny the positive aspects of the word *dialogue* in so far as it refers to an exchange which takes place between human beings, some of whom are Christian and some Muslim.

What do you think you have received from your encounters with Muslims?

It is obvious that we are living in a society where faith is almost natural. So one cannot forget God's presence in the life of the world when one is in a Muslim society where the reference to God is continuous. There is the practice of prayer five times a day. But also there is the practice of daily life where people place themselves before God, maintain their fidelity to God, try to know God's will for them, and so on. These public manifestations of faith are a support to Christians in their personal relationship with God, even if the nature of the Christian relationship to God is different from that of the Muslim. But the fact of being in a society where faith in the existence of God is natural creates a different environment from that which one finds in Western societies where very often God's face is absent from daily life.

Muslim societies also have a certain number of fraternal values that are no longer very present in the West, such as the value of hospitality, family solidarity, respect for the young and for the elderly. These values challenge Christians to be faithful to the commands of Jesus, "Love your neighbor as yourself" and "Love one another as I have loved you." But we find this fraternity within the Muslim community even if there are also rifts, jealousies, dishonesty, and so on. Respect for the elderly is a value that is unquestionably present in Algerian society and makes us question what is happening in Western societies. Jesus tells us that God is love; humanity does not find its true vocation unless people remain in love and God will then remain in them. As Christians in Algerian society, we are happy to live this message. We have there a specifically Christian motivation that is perhaps theologically more affirmed than in Islam and mystically more at the center of the believer's fidelity to God.

Do Christians offer Muslims an understanding of God's love?

I think that Muslims can understand this when they are sufficiently close to us, for example, that Christian prayer is a filial relationship with God long before it is an obligation expressed through gestures, rites, and so on. Also, they can understand, especially through the work of the sisters, that fidelity to God is fidelity to the service of the poor—disabled people, old people, all those who are in difficult situations. Thus there is a subtle process of osmosis that leads a large number of Algerians to see their fidelity to God not merely as a response to the verses of the Qur'an or the requirements of Islamic law, but mainly in light of what their conscience tells them about the nature of the good. One must *do* good, of course, but what is this goodness? So the Islamic conscience is influenced, to some extent, by the actions of Christians.

I have been struck, perhaps naïvely, by the evangelical language of the young Muslims whom I have met, for example, "We are all brothers"; "Act in a brotherly manner"; and so forth.

In reality one must understand that they have two sets of references. These expressions affirming fraternity are what they sincerely believe when they are with us. But when they go back to their communities, they habitually hear a discourse in which the Muslim is a brother of the Muslim, where the community referred to is the Muslim community, where the fidelity is one owed to Muslims and Islam and where fairly often Christians and Jews are considered with distrust, even regarded as infidels. The discourse that they use in their relationships with us when they are close to us is sincere, but it comes up against another form of discourse that is addressed to them and that inevitably influences them. It is one of the objectives of encounter to ensure that the discourse of mutual exclusion of communities doesn't become the only discourse and that another question arises: Are we not all brothers despite the fact that some are Christians and others are Muslims?

A final question. Before long you will be retiring. What is your hope for the Algerian Church?

My hope is that the relations that exist, which are built on one hundred and fifty years of encounter between Christian and Muslim, may develop and deepen. I hope that the discourse of exclusion that continues, unfortunately, to be proclaimed by many religious circles within the Algerian Muslim community will be at last denounced by the Muslims themselves and that they will end up saying to those in charge of their mosques: "We don't recognize ourselves in what you say about Islam, about the rest of the world. We do not wish to divide the world between the faithful whom God loves and the infidels whom we must distrust, fight, and even drive from our national soil." And that thus, little by little, loyal people can challenge each other. There are also those who become Christian, and this is of course a joy, but to define the existence of the Church here solely by a few baptisms is to completely miss the important question: What have we got to do when we are Christian and the others are Muslim and remain Muslim? We are not going to define our responsibility solely by the fact that out of one hundred thousand Muslims there is one who becomes Christian. We have got to be interested in what we can give to each other. In the vast majority of cases the Muslim remains Muslim, the Christian remains Christian. Is it a question of two communities living in watertight compartments or have they something to give each other? I hope in the future that this vocation of ours will become a reality.

Appendices

Appendix A: Reflections of Msgr. Teissier

This appendix features three addresses by Msgr. Teissier on the witness given by the Algerian Church through her relationship with Muslim people. I have translated them from the French.

Address One: To Offer One's Life out of Love

The Holy Father has asked that during the Jubilee Year a celebration be organized in the Coliseum in memory of the new martyrs, those of the twentieth century. He fixed May 7 as the date for this celebration. We know that this century has known, more than any other, bloody persecutions of the Christian community. We have had the martyrs of communist atheism in the Soviet Union, in China, in Vietnam, and in many other countries. We have had the martyrs of Nazism and those of the Spanish war. We have had the martyrs of Central Africa (Rwanda, Congo, Burundi), and those who, as in Latin America, gave their lives in solidarity with the poor peasants, victims of systems based upon money and power.

In this long list of victims the group of religious from Algeria occupy a special place. Indeed, they make up only a small number in comparison with all the victims from Algeria, and even more so in comparison with the great persecutions that we have just cited. In the Soviet Union, for example, about a million Christian martyrs were put to death for their faith. But what is special about the members of the religious orders, victims of violence in Algeria, is that they were led to give their lives, not in order to avoid denying their faith, nor to defend a Christian community but out of evangelical fidelity to a Muslim people.

Fidelity to a Muslim People

The nineteen religious martyred in Algeria were in fact subjected to this out of fidelity to an ecclesial vocation to serve and love a Muslim people. They had not remained in Algeria to support a Christian community. The majority of Christians had, in fact, been led to leave the country as the Algerian fundamentalism progressively became more radical. Our martyrs are part of that little group of religious and laypeople who had stayed on in Algeria out of fidelity to a Muslim people. Each one of them had recognized their vocation in the call that the Algerian Church had addressed to them, to draw close to brothers and sisters who were Muslims and who intended to remain so.

It is important to highlight this special vocation. In answer to the call of the Church of Vatican II, these religious had given up the joy of serving a Christian community in their own countries. They had even given up the joy, deeper still, of working as missionaries in a part of the world where, by God's grace, catechumens are numerous and give birth to a new Church.

These martyrs believed in the Word of the Church at the end of the twentieth century, which sent them to search out brothers and sisters to love among the believers of Islam. They believed, with the Church of Vatican II, that God could send them to share spiritually in a way which would go beyond the divisions between Islam and Christianity. They believed that the Kingdom of God can be announced even to brothers and sisters who intend to remain outside Christianity but who are open to a sharing of God's gift, which goes beyond religious differences. They believed that there are also human and religious fidelities in the house of Islam. Doesn't God's Spirit act in every upright conscience so that it brings forth the fruits of the Kingdom?

Working for the Kingdom

They also believed that the task of reconciling Christian and Muslim, after centuries of fratricidal struggles, is part of the work of the Kingdom of God. They believed that service of the poor, of women in difficult circumstances, of the handicapped, of youth, is service of the Lord Jesus, even if these poor, these women, these youth are Muslim. They wished to show these Muslim brothers and sisters that one can give one's life for them because God invites us to love one another and that this commandment is more important than our religious differences. In the parable of the Good Samaritan—the parable of charity—Jesus chose to take the example of a loving relationship that goes beyond religious differences. The love that God invites us to live ought to go beyond all religious, racial, or cultural barriers.

When the crisis worsened it would have been possible for our martyrs to leave a country where they had no Christian community to defend. But they had the conviction that their love for their Muslim brothers and sisters ought to go as far as the risk they had assumed, out of love. It was their way of remaining faithful to the Gospel of universal brotherhood.

The Marist brother, Henri Vergès, and the Little Sister of the Assumption, Paul-Hélène, remained with the eleventh and twelfth graders in the poor neighborhood of the Kasbah, and they were victims of their fidelity to these young people. That was May 8, 1994, eight years ago. The Spanish Augustinian Missionary Sisters were faithful to the inhabitants of their working class neighborhood of Bab-el-Oued, and they were victims of the violence, at the door of the chapel of their neighborhood. Likewise the four White Fathers from Tizi-Ouzou, wishing to remain faithful to the population of their region, remained in Kabylia, and the Sisters of Our Lady of the Apostles also continued with their work in their Belcourt neighborhood. The Little Sister Odette wished to remain faithful to her Kouba neighbors and the seven monks to the farmers of Tibhirine. And it is also out of fidelity to his people, Christian and Muslim together, that Fr. Claverie remained at his post as bishop even though he knew he was under threat.

The Teaching of St. Augustine

One can highlight the specific motivation of our martyrs by comparing their generosity of spirit to that evoked by St. Augustine, faced by the violence of his era. In 430, at a time when the Vandals were making progress in North Africa, St. Augustine was questioned by two of his bishops, first by a certain Quodvultdeus, and then by Honoratus, who had just been ordained to serve a town adjacent to Thagaste. These two bishops wondered if it wouldn't be better for the clergy to shelter from the Vandal menace so that they would be able to serve again once the crisis had passed. Augustine replied that the good shepherd lays down his life for his flock, that the pastors cannot leave in the hour of need unless their flock itself chooses to flee.

Augustine was in this case talking about the fidelity of the pastor to his Christian flock. The Vatican II Church sent out martyrs to serve a non-Christian people. And these priests and religious felt bound by the same fidelity as if their people were Christian. The immense family of God's children for whom one can lay down one's life goes beyond all confessional, cultural, or ethnic barriers.

This evolution has, moreover, been noticed by many of our Muslim friends. They felt wounded by the attacks against us as if they were part of the Christian family. Or, rather, they felt wounded because they were part of the family of the Kingdom, despite being non-Christian.

Fr. Christian's testament allows us to understand the interior motivation that inspired all of them and that brought them close to all their Muslim Algerian brothers and sisters, victims of the same violence. He shows us an evangelical love which knows no boundaries, a love which the Church of Vatican II sees as a concern not only of Algerian Christians but also of the Church of our time. By incarnating himself in our humanity two thousand years ago, the Word of God united himself to all of humanity. We must from now on recognize and serve him in every person, even to the point of laying down our lives. Do we not find in this martyrdom an evangelical fidelity to a humanity without boundaries?

+Henri Teissier, Editorial in
La Semaine Religieuse d'Alger 5 (2002)

Address Two : A Church Without Christians Which Is the Church of a Muslim People

The first characteristic of our Algerian Church which one needs to understand can be expressed as follows, "We are a Church without laity." We are a Church because we have four bishops for the four major regions of Algeria, 110 priests or religious, two hundred sisters, and a few hundred lay missionaries. But we are a Church without Christians because the totality of the Algerian people is Muslim.

The second characteristic of our Algerian Church is that she is the Church of a people, despite lacking a body of lay faithful. But this people is Muslim. We find ourselves scattered among them over all of the country—from Tamanrasset, Tazrouk, and Assekrem, two thousand kilometers to the south—and as far as Algiers, Oran, and Annaba (the former Hippo of St. Augustine) on the edge of the Mediterranean. We are the Church of a Muslim people because we are to be found with them—from Tébessa; Bir el Ater; Souk Ahras (the former Tagaste), the city where St. Augustine was born, along the Tunisian border—and as far as Tlemcen, Tounane, and Ghazaouët, a thousand kilometers to the west, along the Moroccan border. We are the Church of a Muslim people and we are to be found with them in the regional capitals like Algiers, Oran, Constantine, and Annaba but also in the small coastal cities such as Béjaïa, Skikda, or Ténès; in the Atlas mountains in Lakhdaria, Tablat, Mascara, or Hennaya; or in the high plateaux in places like Chéchar, Laghouat, El Abiod Sidi-Cheikh; and in the oases such as Touggourt, Ouargla, El Goléa, or Timimoun.

In each of these locations the few Christian laypeople, priests, and sisters are in the midst of an entirely Muslim population. They wish to be in relationship with these people, in solidarity with them, at their service in the dialogue of daily life and of prayer.

The Places of Solidarity of Our Church with the Muslim Population

We cannot make progress in the discovery of the reality of our Church without being very clear about these very special circumstances. We are accustomed to calculating the number of priests and religious in a Church in relation to the number of laity. Our circumstances are very different. Priests, religious, and laity— there are a few hundred of us at the most, or if you include the technicians at the petroleum sites and the African students, a few thousand Christians. But all of these Christians have no other reason for being there, from a human and spiritual point of view, other than to live and collaborate with the local people who are entirely made up of Muslims.

Different people live this relationship according to their own circumstances: the technicians in their working relationship with their Muslim colleagues; the Christian teachers (mainly priests who speak Arabic) in their relationship with their Muslim partners; the Christian health workers (mainly sisters) in their work with Muslim patients and with the Muslim hospital administrators; the specialized educators of the young handicapped in their relationship with Muslim educators and with the Muslim parents of the children.

However, Christians live out this relationship with Islam and with Muslims through their own particular circumstances or according to the charism of their congregations. The Jesuits have libraries at the service of Muslim students; the Little Sisters of the Poor have houses for elderly Muslims which they run with the financial help of Muslim families. The Little Sisters of Jesus have Muslim neighbors with whom they have daily relationships. *Caritas* works with Muslim voluntary associations. If sisters have a sewing school, it is for young Muslim girls or for a Muslim municipality or an association of Muslim parents. The parish libraries are open to Muslim neighbors. The Diocesan House youth club is made up of young Muslims with Muslim youth workers. The choir which came to sing in our chapel to bring us a little joy after Easter is made up of young singers, all of whom are Muslim. Those attending lectures which we organize are almost all Muslims, with the exception of some priests and religious. Our brother monks of Tibhirine used to live among Muslims and prayed for Muslim neighbors. Even the people who come to see us in the bishops' offices are in the majority Muslim, and those whom I invite to my table as friends to share a meal—apart from priests and religious—are all Muslims. As for the few Algerian Christians, it's even simpler still. They are in solidarity with all of their families, who are Muslim.

Christians and Muslims, Common Tasks

Of course, these Muslims whom we meet do not usually come to see us in order to establish a Christian-Muslim dialogue. They come to see us because we wish to be men and women of solidarity. If the parents of a handicapped child come to see us, it is to find an educational solution that will benefit their child. They know that we will show concern and that we will seek together to find a practical solution, for example, to start up a voluntary association for parents of handicapped children. If women come to see us because they want to find a way of ensuring greater respect for women, for their dignity, and their role in society, they know that we are concerned by the questions that they are raising. We will seek together a solution in partnership with the Muslim women's associations that we know and that are already working to achieve the same end. If young Muslim graduates come to see us because they have been unable to find work, they know that we will seek together to discover employment schemes or how to set them up if they do not exist. If those in charge of social or cultural associations come to see us, they know that we share their passion, whether it be for serving their brothers and sisters or for the cultural well-being of all. And they are happy to find in us interlocutors who are passionate about what they are doing.

Christians and Muslims, Common Sorrows and Joys

All the more if someone comes to see us because they have lost a father, or a son, or a spouse, or a sister on account of the violence that is widespread in the country, they know that we will share their suffering and that we will help them to hold on to hope when all human hope has vanished. If people come to see us because they fail to understand how one can kill in the name of God, and sometimes kill two-year-old children or disabled elderly people, they also know that they can talk to us about their bewilderment and that we can seek together, with respect for their convictions, what our response should be to violence in God's name. And it is likewise for all the questioning which is a part of people's lives during a time of crisis such as the country is experiencing. They know that we can speak together about the consequences for family life of the economic crisis; they know that we, like them, are aware of the brutal nature of market forces and of liberal capitalism. They have even more reason to wonder about the relationships between men and women, parents and children, about the relation between the state and personal freedom, about the relationship between religious duty and the personal responsibility of individual conscience, about the pluralism of religious traditions, about the differences and similarities that keep them apart and draw them together. And finally, beyond all that, we can share our questions about discovering the true face of God and about the meaning of every human life.

Christians and Muslims, Overcoming Prejudice Together

For fourteen centuries, with a few exceptions, Christians and Muslims in North Africa have long considered themselves as belonging to two opposing camps. The situation is not exactly the same in the Middle East, where there exist Christians and Muslims who belong to the same country and the same culture, as in Egypt, Syria, Palestine, Lebanon, Iraq. In Algeria, the ancient Christian community (that of the time of St. Augustine with six hundred dioceses from Cyrenaica to Tingitane Mauritania) disappeared in the wake of the Arab-Muslim conquest between the eighth and the eleventh centuries. The Almohad Empire finally ordered the suppression of the last surviving Jews or Christians in the twelfth century.

Next came the Corsair war between the north and south of the Mediterranean, despite the commercial relations which a few courageous navigators succeeded in maintaining, and this was followed by the colonial conquest. From that time on the Christian is seen here not simply as the foreigner but primarily as the historic enemy. It is different in black Africa where one can find in the same family Christians and Muslims. Here the Algerian who becomes a Christian—and there were some during the colonial period—is seen as someone who has changed sides. Muslim apologetics has developed a routine discourse which devalues the Christian and his tradition. The official propaganda designates the West—and through it the Christian world—as enemy territory.

Christians and Muslims, Showing Solidarity

Now that the Christians of European origin have all departed, our little group is seen less as the representative of another side than as brothers and sisters who are different and who wish to show solidarity. The differences between us remain but the prejudices are challenged because we find ourselves united in the search for solutions to common problems.

And then everyone knows that if we had wanted to leave we could have done so. It is well known that ever since turmoil struck the country, our embassies have insisted that we should leave. And as you see we have remained and remain while almost all of the Christian families have left. And thus we find ourselves in even deeper solidarity. Of course, this is not generally the case. There are first of all the Algerians who never meet us, who think that we have left, and who are astonished when they do meet us. There is the small minority who think that we have no right to be in the country and who wish to see us leave. Among this group are the fanatics who have killed nineteen of us to make us understand that we *should* leave. But precisely on account of these very attacks, there are those who show us even more solidarity because a threat to us is a threat to them—they have a different understanding of Islam, a different understanding of life in society. Thus, those very people who are threatening us in order to cut us off from society are in fact bringing us closer to the vast majority of those who know us, who condemn these crimes, and who are now committing themselves more resolutely than ever to a vision of Islam which is open to "the other," the one who is different.

Must One Persevere Even to Martyrdom?

The kidnapping and subsequent massacre of our seven brother monks has made many people ask us a straightforward question: Should one persevere even to martyrdom? To tell the truth, the monks had asked themselves this question especially, after the assassination of our first brothers and sisters, victims of this violence. And they clearly stated that they didn't wish an Algerian to be responsible for their death. Fr. Christian wrote: "It is very clear that we cannot wish for such a death, not only because we are afraid of it but because we cannot wish for a glory (that of martyrdom) which would be acquired at the price of murder…I love all Algerians enough not to wish that a single one of them should be the Cain of his brother." And the Fr. Prior of Tibhirine returns to this theme in his testament: "I could never wish for such a death…I don't see how I could in fact rejoice that this people whom I love should be accused indiscriminately of my murder."

Moreover, in all the places where the threat of assassination was explicit, we carried out a spiritual discernment with the persons concerned which led them to leave their surroundings or to change their lifestyle. The monks themselves had in principle accepted the possibility of leaving their monastery if the threat became too explicit. This prudence does not prevent us accepting, along with everyone else, the routine risks which a violent situation involves. Most of the religious congregations, especially the female ones, asked their members for a written reflection, personal and secret, which established each person's reasons for assuming the risks involved. The question "Should one persevere even to martyrdom?" is poorly formulated. It would be better to say: There are situations where one must persevere while accepting the risk of becoming a victim of the unjust violence that can make death a witness—a martyrdom.

The Reasons for Our Witness

The presentation which has been given of the state of our Church must now be illuminated by a presentation of the motivation for our witness. The love of God is universal, "who desires everyone to be saved and to come to the knowledge of the truth" (1 Tim 2:4). There is therefore a dialogue of salvation to be undertaken with all the peoples of the earth. "This universal dialogue of salvation" is necessary for the Church herself, who would be unfaithful to her mission if she wasn't its servant. "Go therefore and make disciples of all nations" (Matt 28:19). For a long time this sending out on mission was only understood under its catechumenal aspect, "baptizing them in the name of the Father and of the Son and of the Holy Spirit." Since the beginning of the twentieth century, and especially since Vatican II, the Church has better understood that believers from other religions are also brothers and sisters whom we encounter in order to live together the "dialogue of salvation." The Sermon on the Mount gives us, from this perspective, another missionary motivation. "And if you greet only your brothers and sisters, what more are you doing than others? Do not even the Gentiles do the same?" (Matt 5:47). One could gloss it thus, "And if you greet only those whom you are going to baptize what are you doing more than others?"

The sending forth to baptize, as it is presented at the end of Matthew, isn't the only starting place that the Church has for reflecting on her mission. Let us recall the parable of the Final Judgment where the nations will not be judged according to their baptism but according to their openness to their brothers and sisters, "for I was hungry and you gave me food" (Matt 25:35). Let us think in particular of this beatitude, "I was a stranger and you welcomed me" (Matt 25:35). In the relationship with the other, if it is genuine, there is liberation and an entry into the realm of love which is a gift from God. It is in this mutual openness that God brings in his Kingdom. "The Kingdom…grows gradually as people slowly learn to love, forgive and serve one another."[1] These theological certainties become for us experiential realities. Through our collaboration, we perceive prejudices fading, reconciliation taking place, a mutual recognition happening. God thus frees us by means of each other from our imprisonment in our particular group—even should it be the Church—and opens us to his Universal Love.

We have experienced more than ever this new aspect of Mission since the country's independence has scaled down our presence to that of very small groups in the midst of Muslim partners. But this discovery of a new sphere of mission is, in Algeria, older than Vatican II. One has only to think, for example, of Charles de Foucauld at the start of the twentieth century and of his spiritual movement, which spread especially from the middle of that century in Algeria and from this country to the whole world. In Italy this message has often become known through Carlo Caretto. It is a matter of discovering new aspects of the universal action of the Holy Spirit. The Spirit is at work in all people, opening their hearts to the values of the Kingdom and bringing to birth in each one the spiritual attitudes which Jesus showed in his life and in his Gospel. The March 1997 declaration of the International Theological Commission provides us with the most recent doctrinal context in which to understand these missionary perspectives.[2]

A Martyred Church through Fidelity to a Muslim People

In 430, Honoratus, bishop of Thiana near Tagaste (today Souk Ahras) wrote a letter to St. Augustine asking him how Christian pastors should respond to the approach of the Vandals, who were sacking everything in their path. Should they not leave to return later once the danger had passed? Augustine replied with a little treatise where he expounded this conviction, "One should not abandon the Church which we must serve."[3] Augustine was giving in this instance instructions to pastors on remaining faithful to the Christian community. The evolution in theological thought that we have just discussed has made us become not the pastors but the partners of a non-Christian people who are the people of our Church, the people whom the Universal Church has entrusted to us. Most of the priests of our Church, a large number of religious, and a few mostly celibate lay missionaries have had the inner conviction that their involvement in the dialogue of salvation with their Muslim Algerian brothers and sisters involves the same obligation of faithfulness as that which pastors had to their Christian communities in the time of Augustine.

All of our missionary vocation has been committed for years, in truth for decades, to this spiritual certainty that God has chosen us to be the Christian partners of a Muslim people. Through this relationship we experience the Master of the Harvest bringing about his Kingdom and empowering the dialogue of salvation. To depart in time of danger, if it is not absolutely necessary, would be at odds with this spiritual solidarity which we live with our Muslim partners and which is our vocation as persons and as Church. This was the issue for our brother monks of Our Lady of Atlas, who couldn't conceive of abandoning their Muslim neighbors of the little village of Tibhirine in the Médéa region.

We can say the same thing about our other brothers and sisters: Br. Henri Vergès and the Little Sister of the Assumption, Paul-Hélène Saint Raymond, faithful to the youth of the Kasbah whom they served; the Augustinian sisters Esther and Caridad, faithful to the handicapped of Ben Aknoun and to the inhabitants of Bab-el-Oued; the four White Fathers of Tizi-Ouzou, faithful to the people of Kabylia, where their Congregation had served for more than a century; the two sisters of Our Lady of the Apostles, Bibiane and Angèle-Marie, faithful to the young girls of the Belcourt district in Algiers; sister Odette, faithful to her district of Apreval in Kouba, a suburb of Algiers; and Pierre Claverie, faithful both to his Christian people in Oran and to the population of the city and of the region.

This witness has been noticed by our Algerian friends. As you know, the Qur'an denies that Jesus was crucified. Allying itself with a Christian docetic stream of thought in the first centuries, Islam teaches that at the last moment God substituted for Jesus another man who died in his place. For us Christians such a perspective is in total contradiction with everything Jesus had to say, "I lay down my life for the sheep" (John 10:15). There is therefore in the following of Christ an identification with his sacrifice in the lives of all those who enter into communion with Jesus' offering, by taking the risk of loving their brothers and sisters at the peril of their own lives.

As Fr. Christian of Tibhirine remarked, it is not a question in our context of a martyrdom of faith, a story told by the first centuries of Christian life, but of a martyrdom of charity. Fr. Christian takes the example of Maximillian Kolbe as particularly expressive of this message, "to give one's life for one's brothers and sisters." But the twentieth century has known many other examples of this martyrdom of charity, in Latin America or Rwanda or Zaire where so many pastors, religious and laity have become victims of their solidarity with a people, a solidarity lived out of an evangelical motivation as a response to their being sent on mission by the Church *to* this people, *with* this people.

A Church That Must Live Beyond Martyrdom

However, our martyred brothers and sisters have not only left us the witness of their death; they have also handed down to us the message of their lives, which were made up of an evangelical fidelity to a people. Beyond the great suffering that has deprived us of their physical presence by our side, we welcome their message. We wish to continue to live this mission of being the Church of a Muslim people. This mission, moreover, becomes daily more significant because there are many Muslims today who go from the "you and we," which separates and leads to opposition, to the "we," which draws us closer together. Thus more and more we see ourselves as "they and we," as brothers and sisters with a common humanity devoted to the same tasks of the future. It is a matter of constructing a new society where we can discover that we are related and members of the same family, under the eyes of God, despite the prejudices of history, the barriers of dogma and the violence of fanatics.

After the first attack against our community, Algerian friends of the first two religious who were victims of the crisis expressed this hope in the following way:

> We A.B., journalist, and M.M., a university teacher, would like to manifest our friendship and fraternity with you in this drama which affects all of us today. *As for us, never forget that you are forever our brothers and sisters.* Whatever our differences of dogma, we believe that we have the same God. And, let's be clear about it, we love you and that concerns no one else. Once more, contrary to the assassins, we say to you: you are at home here, we love you and we pray beside you for the repose of the soul of those who have been slaughtered in a cowardly fashion. We dare to remind you that in Notre-Dame d'Afrique, there is inscribed above the Black Virgin, "Pray for us and for Muslims."

An evolution is taking place here whose full meaning must be grasped. Christians are assassinated by Muslims in the name of their understanding of Islam. Following this, other Muslims feel themselves closer to the Christian victims and to their friends than to the Muslim assassins. The most recent attacks in Egypt against Coptic Christians have aroused the same reactions.

From now on what counts is no longer which religion one belongs to, but how one understands one's religion. If it is a religion that excludes the other, we want to have nothing to do with it. If it is a religion that respects the other, a respect that expresses itself through fidelity to God and to his will, we recognize ourselves as being close and we become close. Are we not in the realm of that religion "in spirit and in truth" which Jesus announced to the Samaritan woman?

The Algerian Church

A hundred years ago the emigration of a European people and of a European population to the south of the Mediterranean brought about the birth of a Church in Algeria. But this Church was, in fact, concerned above all by pastoral work with Christians of European origin. That is why in 1868, when Cardinal Lavigerie founded the White Fathers and the White Sisters, he forbade them to make contact with the European parishes. He sent them into the country regions and to the Muslim districts. Finally, at the end of the colonial period and more particularly with the major crisis in society, all the inhabitants of European origin left. There only remained a few people with a strong evangelical motivation. They are not here to establish a Church in Algeria, but to be the Algerian Church, the Church of Algeria, the Church of a Muslim people. It is the Church of Vatican II concerned about "the joys and hopes, the grief and anguish of the people of our time" (G.S. 1).[4] When the Pope goes to Sarajevo or to Beirut, he doesn't go there to meet only the Christians of Bosnia or the Lebanon. He goes there to draw close also to all of the Bosnian people or to all of the Lebanese people. For the Love of God is universal and the Church is a sign and a servant of this Love.

Note: This address was given by Msgr. Teissier in Italian to a missionary Congress held in Brescia, Italy on May 17, 1997.

Address Three: Proclaiming the Gospel to Our Muslim Partners

In the context of Christian-Muslim relations, many are wondering if a "proclamation of the Gospel" is possible and if so, how? Through the following suggestions I would like to explore some possibilities in this area. It is obvious that in Muslim countries there are no satisfying answers to the question posed, "What proclamation?" if we have only one understanding of what "proclamation" means. It would undoubtedly be difficult to apply to the witness of Christians living in a Muslim society forms of witness that have been lived out in other parts of the globe. To proclaim the Gospel, is, it seems to me, to show forth the life of Jesus in our own life. Christ is the sign of God's presence among us and the principal actor of the Kingdom of which we are all servants. How can we show forth the reality of God's gift in Jesus Christ today as Christians in a Muslim society?

1. To Proclaim my Christian Identity

Every Christian life proclaims the Lord Jesus, especially in a Muslim country. Our Muslim neighbors know straightaway that we are Christian because in a Muslim country one cannot hide one's religious identity—except in the special case of Muslim converts to Christianity, who are condemned, almost everywhere, to live their Christian faith in secret.

Muslims in Arab countries almost always try to find out if the person to whom they are speaking is or isn't a Muslim. A Christian's behavior represents Christianity in the eyes of Muslims, whether the Christian wishes it or not. That is why even Christians who no longer have any contact with the Church are looked upon as representing Christianity. One speaks at times of a simple presence. There is no such thing as a simple presence. Christians carry their identity with them, revealing what it means to be Christian. By merely being a Christian, one becomes a witness of the Christian faith before Muslims. Thus every encounter of a Christian with a Muslim is already a proclamation. Through our presence as Christians among Muslims, we proclaim that Christianity is still alive and that it still animates the life of believers who are not Muslims. But we need to go further and discover together the characteristics of our Christian identity that come into play in this encounter.

2. The Christian is a Person of Reconciliation and of Peace

In the Christian-Muslim relationship we must go beyond a troubled past. For fourteen centuries, at least in the Mediterranean area, Christian and Muslim confronted each other. The colonial dominance and the Palestinian problem have worsened this relationship. New conflicts can appear at any moment. We saw this with September 11. This could also happen with a new attack against Iraq. The work of reconciliation is far from being complete and it always requires us to start afresh.

According to St. Luke (10:5), Jesus sent forth his apostles with these words: "Whatever house you enter, first say, 'Peace to this house!'" I underscore the word *first*. The Gospel workers do not come to stir up war and conflicts, even if Jesus tells us that the missionary may know hostility. St. Paul says that Jesus came to overcome hate. "So he came and proclaimed peace to you who were far off and peace to those who were near" (Eph 2:17). Undoubtedly when Paul speaks, he wishes first of all to describe the peace which, through a collective conversion to the Gospel, will gather together Jew and Gentile into the family of the Father. But Jesus also says to us, "And if you greet only your brothers and sisters, what more are you doing than others? Do not even the Gentiles do the same?" (Matt 5:47). The Sermon on the Mount is clear, "Love your enemies and pray for those who persecute you…For if you love those who love you, what reward do you have?" (Matt 5:44, 46). Moreover Christian prayer tells us, "Forgive us our trespasses as we forgive those who trespass against us" (cf. Matt 6:12). The first proclamation of a Christian meeting a Muslim must be that of peace. By doing that, the Christian works for reconciliation. It is already to proclaim the God whom we serve, who gathers together in his love all his scattered children.

3. The Christian Is a Person Who Respects Others in Their Personal and Communal Identities

There will be no reconciliation without respect for others in their personal and communal identities. This respect is part of all Christian fidelity. Jesus invites us to discover his image in the face of every person. "I was a stranger and you welcomed me, I was naked and you gave me clothing, sick and you took care of me, I was in prison and you visited me…. 'Truly I tell you, just as you did it to one of the least of these who are members of my family, you did it to me'" (Matt 25:35–36, 40). Let us recall Jesus' invitation to respect every human being, even the little ones whose "angels continually see the face of my Father in heaven" (Matt 18:11). Nothing keeps people further apart than contempt. Contempt destroys the other, striking at their personal identity as well as their communal identity. Nothing draws people closer than respect. "So it is not the will of your Father in heaven that one of these little ones should be lost" (Matt 18:14).

4. The Christian Is a Person Who Draws Close

Jesus made the parable of the Good Samaritan the sign of fidelity to God. We know that Jesus concludes the parable by asking, "'Which of these three, do you think, was a neighbor to the man who fell into the hands of the robbers?' He said, 'The one who showed him mercy.' Jesus said to him, 'Go, and do likewise'" (Luke 10:36–37).

Too often our definition of mission is limited to the command that comes at the end of Matthew, "Go therefore and make disciples of all nations, baptizing them in the name of the Father and of the Son and of the Holy Spirit" (28:19). To make Gospel disciples of all nations is to remember what Jesus says at the end of the parable of the Good Samaritan, "Go, and do likewise" (Luke 10:37). Teach that to everyone as a life principle valid for all, but above all as a way of living which is learnt first of all by example. "Go, and do likewise, draw close to those from whom you could have remained distant." Isn't this one of the characteristics of mission? To draw close to those from whom we could have remained distant and all of this on account of Jesus Christ and his Gospel, on account of the love of God which draws close. It is the very movement of the incarnation which is taken up again by mission.

5. To Love Our Brothers and Sisters in Order to Reveal the Love of God

Jesus, according to Matthew, replies to the question about the greatest commandment by this sentence, "You shall love the Lord your God...This is the greatest and the first commandment" and he adds, "And a second is like it, 'You shall love your neighbor as yourself'" (Matt 22:37–39). We know how St. John deepened this teaching of Jesus, "Everyone who loves is born of God and knows

God...for God is love" (1 John 4:7–8). The heart of Christian Revelation is there. Mission is the Revelation of the love which God has shown to us in Jesus Christ. Christian life, if it is faithful, welcomes this love of God in order to live from it.

To think about "proclamation" in our relationships with our Muslim friends is to think about how effectively our lives witness to love. This message is made clear to our Muslim friends when they realize that love is at the heart of Christian fidelity to God, for God is love and sends us forth to manifest love to one another. Of course, our Muslim friends do not use the specifically Christian language of love that has its roots in the Trinitarian communion. Love for a Christian is the substance of the Divinity through the communion of persons. But Muslims who are, for example, close to a community of religious sisters can very well understand that the sisters have a mission to "do good to people and to the little ones." And they can understand that such an attitude is at the heart of the sisters' religious faith. In this way, Christians can proclaim that God is love and that the truly faithful ones are those who love their brothers and sisters. "By this everyone will know that you are my disciples, if you have love for one another" (John 13:35). "You have but one teacher, and you are all brothers" (Matt 23:8, NAB).

6. Jesus the Servant of God

Love takes many forms, for example, conjugal love, paternal love, pastoral love, friendship, and so on. But among the specifically evangelical forms of love, there is that of service. Jesus applied to himself the Song of the Servant. As Servant he lays down his life for his people. "For the Son of Man came not to be served but to serve" (Mark 10:45). "So if I, your Lord and Teacher, have washed your feet, you also ought to wash one another's feet. For I have set you an example, that you also should do as I have done to you" (John

13:14–15). To freely take the attitude of a servant, is to show that service is a sign of the presence of God among humankind, it is to show the face which God has given to us of himself in Jesus Christ.

7. The Universality and Gratuitousness of Evangelical Love

The love that reveals God is not any old sentiment. It has at least two characteristic features. It is universal and free. To love only those who are the same as oneself is in the end to love only oneself. But to love without erecting boundaries is to respond to the Sermon on the Mount. "For if you love those who love you, what reward do you have? Do not even the tax collectors do the same?" (Matt 5:46). The love that reveals the God of the Gospel is one which makes no distinction between people. It is for this reason that Jesus chose the parable of the Good Samaritan to speak to us about God's way of loving. The Samaritan cares for the wounded Jew. It is moreover what Jesus himself lived out. His love is universal and free. The God of Jesus Christ "makes his sun to rise on the evil and on the good" (Matt 5:45).

Conclusion

It is obvious that in a relationship with Muslim partners it is problematic to introduce Christian ideas that are contrary to Islam. To tackle these themes is almost always to end up in controversy, which isn't the work of the Spirit. On the other hand, to choose the path of reconciliation, of peace, of mutual respect, of love which serves and doesn't make distinctions shows God's love and leads the Muslim partner towards specifically Christian values. The Muslim partner cannot recognize in the incarnation or the trinity the path to God. On the other hand, in reconciliation, respect, service and universal, free love they recognize a gift of God. When they know the Christian identity of the person who lives out this love, they recognize that it is God who is the author of this gift. They make themselves then, even unknown to themselves, close to the God of Jesus Christ at the heart of his mystery: God is love. For Muslims to recognize and savor this mystery is already in itself a fruit of the Spirit of Christ.

Note: This address was given by Msgr. Teissier in Italian at Rome on September 22, 2002, on the occasion of a national colloquium on the subject of migrants.

Appendix B: Ribat es-Salam

This is my own brief account of the history of the Ribat, a Christian-Muslim group engaged in spiritual dialogue.

The Bond of Peace

The effort of Christian and Muslim to understand each other's tradition in Algeria has been particularly fruitful in the work of the Ribat es-Salam ("The Bond of Peace," see Ephesians 4:3). The group held its first meeting on March 24, 1979, at Tibhirine. The two founding members were Msgr. Claude Rault, a White Father, currently Bishop of Laghouat, and Fr. Christian De Chergé of Tibhirine. At first full membership of the group was open only to Christians. Their aim was to live in "spiritual solidarity" with their Muslim brothers and sisters. Writing on the twenty-fifth anniversary of the founding of the group, Claude Rault had this to say: "At the beginning, it's true, we were only a small group of Christians who expressed a desire to share in this way. But we were already living out this solidarity with our Islamic brothers and sisters where we lived and worked, and we were carrying them in our hearts. We also timidly ventured into their Tradition and Book, like children who are learning how to read, to get to know them better. And to know better, isn't it also to love better?"[1]

A Spiritual Solidarity

The group, which almost from the beginning had Muslim participants, meets twice a year, and its members seek to grow closer to each other's tradition without denying their differences. These differences, in the case of the Ribat, do not lead to a "will to dominate" but are rather "places of communion."[2] The first meeting of the Ribat, with seven participants, produced a statement of intent, *Life in communion and call to prayer*.[3] They expressed the wish to establish "a spiritual solidarity with Islam, lived more especially at the level of prayer."[4] The group was conscious of not being representative of their own faith communities, but nevertheless they felt it important that their initiative should be an expression of the Christian Church in Algeria. In their solidarity with Islam they wished to gain nourishment from its spiritual tradition especially through contact with the lowly and humble. The founding members also wished to "seize the opportunity of common prayer, that simple prayer which flows from the heart and which is the gift of the Spirit of God."[5] The group in its founding charter also expressed the desire to remain closely attached to the monastery of Tibhirine, a place where they could draw on "all the sap of the Scriptures and of the Church." This was a wise decision as Christianity in its monastic tradition comes closest to the way of Islam with their common emphasis on communal prayer and communal living.

From its first meeting, the Ribat manifested a very clear desire to draw on the spiritual riches of Islam and to grow closer to the poor and lowly among its followers, those obedient to God. Christian de Chergé, Br. Henri Vergès and others of the Ribat became further immersed in the spirit of Islam through a prayerful reading of the Qur'an. And they were not afraid to pray with their Muslim friends, recognizing that all sincere prayer, whether it be Muslim or Christian, ultimately has its source in God's Spirit. According to Br. Armand Garin, current chairperson of the Ribat, once the Sufi brotherhood began to participate in the Ribat meetings a time of silent prayer became a part of the proceedings.[6] However, efforts by the Christian members to participate in the Muslim times of prayer met with difficulties and were abandoned. A time of silent prayer is now customary with readings from one of the traditions at the beginning or the end of the prayer time. The silence is broken from time to time by a few phrases or verses to avoid too much monotony as not everyone is used to silent prayer. The verses may be either recited or chanted depending on the person in charge and accompanied by a musical instrument such as a flute or harmonium. The essential thing, according to Armand, is that the space and the texts chosen should be acceptable to both groups and not cause either of them to feel any embarrassment.

A Desire for Communion

In a second formulation of the nature and purpose of the Ribat in October 1982, the stress was laid on God's search for man. Humankind's spiritual search for God is a sign of the indwelling Spirit, which is where this longing for God has its origin and goal. "And we recognize that this Spirit is poured out on every person."[7] So the members of the Ribat wish to join others of Islam in a common search for God. "If the Spirit is at the heart of every person, may not every person reveal to us something of the face of God?"[8] The desire for communion with God and with others is common to both Christian and Muslim alike. The Ribat then goes on to set forth its vision for living out this communion more deeply through twice yearly meetings. These two day meetings explore a theme common to both the Qur'an and the Bible which strengthen the members' links with the lowly. The meetings took on a deeper significance in 1980 with the participation of the 'Alaouyines Brothers—a Sufi brotherhood within the mystical tradition of Islam. Each meeting explores a theme that the members have reflected upon and tried to live out in the preceding months. The first theme, selected on March 23, 1981, was "How can we make our way more deeply together towards God?" The theme for April 13, 2005, the first hour of which I was privileged to attend, was "I am looking for his face in the depths of your hearts."

Muslim Membership of the Ribat

An important milestone was reached in November 2000, when the Muslim participants, up until then merely invited guests, became full members of the group. In this meeting it was restated that the group was not primarily a study or theological group. "We stressed that the group was made up of believers who give first place to the spiritual dimension rather than the specifically theological. The latter is not absent, but we do not wish to be a study group. Hence the importance [for new members] of an experience of life, of a spiritual journey, of being rooted in their own tradition: believers who wish to proceed together in the search for the face of God and the acquaintance of believers of the other tradition, whilst being themselves strong in the expression of their own faith."[9]

The sturdy faith required of members of the Ribat can be seen in the cost paid by its members. Six of the nineteen assassinated martyrs belonged to this group: Henri Vergès, Sr. Odette, Christian Chessel, and three Tibhirine monks, Christian, Michel, and Christophe. The communion that they longed for on earth with their Muslim brothers and sisters has now, I trust, been granted to them in its fullness. Meanwhile, the members of the Ribat work for communion in the here and now, convinced in the words of its co-founder, Msgr. Claude Rault that "Islam is the bearer of a spiritual Tradition followed by millions of men and women through which they find intimacy with God and a way in which to construct a better world. We cannot remain on the fringe of such an experience lived by so many friends."[10]

Notes

Foreword

1. Benedict XVI, *Deus Caritas Est,* para 1 (London: Catholic Truth Society, 2006), 3.

Introduction

(The Introduction was written in French and was translated by the author. Translations throughout the book from French into English are the author's.)

1. Michael Ipgrave, ed., *The Road Ahead: A Christian-Muslim Dialogue* (London: Church House Publishing, 2002).

2. Henri Teissier, "A Humble and Courageous Man of God," *Identity* 13 (2002): 3–5.

Chapter One: A Fire Burning Inside

1. The name given to people living in Algeria of European extraction.

2. "14 morts et un blessé," *El Watan,* Algerian daily newspaper, 9 April, 2005: http://www.elwatan.com/2005-04-09-16908.

3. Bernardo Olivera o.c.s.o, *How Far To Follow? The Martyrs of Atlas* (Kalamazoo, MI: Cistercian Publications, 1997), 44.

Chapter Two: Confronted by Death

1. Much of the information in this chapter about the Algerian Church is taken from various articles written by Msgr. Teissier.

2. Benjamin Stora, *Histoire de l'Algérie contemporaine, 1830–1988* (Alger: Casbah Editions, 2004), 14.

3. G. D. Kittler, *The White Fathers* (London: W.H. Allen, 1957), 99 ff.

4. W. F. Burridge, *Destiny Africa* (London: Geoffrey Chapman, 1966), 34.

5. Kittler, 104.

6. Henri Teissier, *Chrétiens En Algérie: Un Partage D'Espérance* (Paris: Desclée De Brouwer, 2002), 61–64.

7. See www.Catholic-Hierarchy.org.

8. These figures do not include the estimated three thousand to ten thousand evangelical Christians, recent converts from Islam. I look at this phenomenon in Chapter 11.

9. Teissier, 48.

10. Wikipedia, Algerian Civil War, 27 October, 2005: http://en.wikipedia.org/wiki/Algerian_Civil_War.

11. "Algeria Report of Eminent Panel," July–August 1998, http://www.un.org/NewLinks/dpi2007/contents.htm, 9.

Chapter Three: Cardinal Duval

1. Marie-Christine Ray, *Le Cardinal DUVAL* (Paris: Les Editions du Cerf, 1998), 27. This book contains a series of interviews with the Cardinal that provide much of the biographical detail contained in this chapter.

2. Denis Gonalez and André Nozière, eds. *Au nom de la Vérité, Algérie 1954–1962,* (Paris: Albin Michel, 2001), 188.

3. Ray, 44. Msgr. Duval's initial impressions of poverty and social injustice were confirmed by the lack of educational opportunities for the native population. In 1945, only 11.5 percent of 1,250,000

school-age Algerian Muslim children were receiving instruction in primary schools. See Benjamin Stora, *Histoire de l'Algérie contemporaine, 1830–1988* (Alger: Casbah Editions, 2004), 109–110.

4. Ray, 36.

5. Ibid., 46.

6. Ibid., 70.

7. Gonalez and Nozière, 17.

8. Ibid., 56.

9. Ibid., 94.

10. Ray, 112.

11. Ibid., 81.

12. Cardinal Léon-Étienne Duval, "Présence Fraternelle," Lettre Pastorale du, Cardinal Duval, Alger, 2 February, 1980. Archives, Diocesan Office, 13, rue Khelifa Boukhalfa, Algiers.

13. Ibid., 5.

14. Ibid., 6.

15. Ray, 146.

16. Ibid., 142.

17. Ibid., 142, 166.

18. Ibid., 79.

19. Ibid., 212.

20. Marie-Christine Ray, *Christian de Chergé* (Paris: Bayard Editions, 1998), 211.

Chapter Four: The Gospel Life of Br. Henri Vergès

1. Alain Delorme and Michel Voute, eds. *du Capcir à la Casbah, vie donnée, sang versé,* (France: 42405 Saint-Chamond, Notre-Dame de l'Hermitage, 1996), 37.

2. Ibid., 66, 109.

3. Robert Masson, *Henri Vergès: Un Chrétien dans la Maison de l'Islam* (Paris: Parole et Silence, 2004), 132.

4. Delorme and Voute, 112.

5. Sister Janet was interviewed by the author in Algiers, April 2006.

6. Delorme and Voute, 58.

7. Masson, 156.

8. Ibid., 157.

9. See Appendix B for a fuller account of this movement.

10. During this time of solitude and loneliness, Br. Henri was greatly supported by the Superior General of the Marists, Br. Basilio Rueda. Their correspondence can be read in *Convergences,* edited by Br. Alain Delorme, and published in 2002 by the Marist Generalate in Rome.

11. Delorme and Voute, 32.

12 Ibid., 28–29.

13. Ibid., 119.

14. Ibid., 159.

15. Interview with the author, Algiers, April 2005.

Chapter Five: Six Lives Given, Six Lives Shared

1. Henri Teissier, *Chrétiens en Algérie—Un Partage D'Espérance,* (Paris: Desclée de Brouwer, 2002), 16.

2. My account in this chapter of the sisters' witness draws mainly on the inspiring book by Robert Masson about the nineteen martyrs, *Jusqu'au bout de La Nuit* (Paris: cerf/Saint-Augustin, 1998) and on interviews that I conducted with Msgr. Teissier (April 2005) and with others who knew the sisters (April 2006). One Algerian Christian who is quoted has asked to remain anonymous.

3. Robert Masson, *Jusqu'au bout de La Nuit* (Paris: cerf/Saint-Augustin, 1998), 25.

4. Ibid., 86.

5. Ibid., 89.

6. Ibid., 97.

7. Ibid., 113.

Chapter Six: Strength in Weakness

1. Jean Fisset, "Chemins de vie au Maghreb," *Voix d'Afrique* 62 (2004): 7.

2. W. F. Burridge, *Destiny Africa* (London: Geoffrey Chapman, 1966), 134.

3. Armand Duval, *C'était une longue fidélité à L'Algérie et au Rwanda* (Paris: Médiaspaul, 1998), 52.

4. Ibid., 54.

5. Ibid., 68.

6. Ibid., 71.

7. Ibid., 72.

8. Ibid., 82.

9. Ibid., 88.

10. Ibid., 104.

11. See Appendix B for a fuller description of this movement.

12. Robert Masson, *Jusqu'au bout de La Nuit* (Paris: cerf/Saint-Augustin, 1998), 140.

13. Duval, 27.

14. Christain Chessel, "La Mission Dans La Faiblesse," *se COMPRENDRE* 95 (1995): 2–6.

15. Armand Duval, 226.

Chapter Seven: A Monastery Set on a Mountainside

1. Robert Masson, *Tibhirine Les Veilleurs de l'Atlas* (Paris: Les Editions du Cerf Saint Augustin, 1997), 40.

2. Ibid., 42.

3. Marie-Christine Ray, *Christine de Chergé prieur de Tibhirine* (Paris: Bayard Editions/Centurion, 1998), 60.

4. Masson, 100.

5. Ibid., 100.

6. Claude Garda, "Les monastère cisterciens d'Algérie," *Collectanea Cisterciensia* 58 (1996): 201–216.

7. The initials "RB" refer to the Rule of Benedict, and the abbreviation "Prol." refers to the prologue to that rule. Quotations are taken from Timothy Fry, ed. *RB 1980* (Collegeville, MN: The Liturgical Press, 1982).

8. Philippe Hémon, "Vers un À-Dieu en-visagé de vous. Témoignage personnel d'un moine sur ses frères du monastère de N. –D. de l'Atlas," *Collectanea Cisterciensia* 58 (1996): 230.

9. *Dieu pour tout jour Chapitres de Père Christian de Chergé à la communauté de Tibhirine (1986–1996),* Les Cahiers de Tibhirine, Abbaye Notre-Dame d'Aiguebelle, 26230 Montjoyer, France. This substantial book of 536 pages is a collection of Fr. Christian's thoughtful and learned thrice-weekly talks to the monastic community at Tibhirine.

10. Bruno Chenu, ed. *Sept vies pour Dieu et l'Algérie* (Paris: Bayard Editions/Centurion, 1996), 82.

11. C.T.R. Hewer, *Understanding Islam* (London: SCM Press, 2006), 88.

12. Henri Sanson, *Dialogue intérieur avec l'islam* (Paris: Centurion, 1990), 190.

13. Masson, 103.

14. Chenu, 149.

15. Ibid., 207.

16. Bruno Chenu, ed., *L'invincible espérance* (Paris: Bayard Editions/Centurion, 1997), 225.

17. Ibid., 228.

18. Bruno Chenu, ed., *Sept vies pour Dieu et l'Algérie,* 169–70.

19. Ibid., 152.

20. Henri Teissier, "Note au sujet de nos sept frères de Tibhirine," 10 September, 1997. Archives, Diocesan Office, 13, rue Khelifa Boukhalfa, Algiers.

21. Ibid., 2.

22. Ibid., 2.

23. Bruno Chenu, ed. *Sept vies pour Dieu et l'Algérie,* 170–71.

24. Ibid., 208.

25. An excellent account of the history of Our Lady of Atlas Monastery, Tibhirine, and of the life of the martyred monks is given by John W. Kaiser in *The Monks of Tibhirine,* (St Martin's Press, New York, 2002).

Chapter Eight: My Life was Given to God and to This Country

1. Bruno Chenu, ed., *L'invincible espérance* (Paris: Bayard Editions/Centurion, 1997), 186.

2. Ibid., 33–38.

3. See Appendix B for a fuller account of this movement.

4. Marie-Christine Ray, *Christian De Chergé* (Paris: Bayard Editions/Centurion, 1998), 148.

5. Chenu, 314.

6. Ibid., 309–10.

7. Ibid., 309.

8. Ibid., 276.

Chapter Nine: A Crucified Love

1. Frère Christophe, *Le Souffle du Don, Journal de frère Christophe, Moine de Tibhirine, 8 Août 1993 – 19 Mars 1996* (Paris: Bayard Editions/Centurion, 1999). All the brief unattributed quotations are from this book and can be located under the date of the journal entry.

2. Henri Quinson, *Prier 15 Jours avec Christophe Lebreton* (91680 Bruyères-le-Châtel, France: Nouvelle Cité, 2007), 11–18. Most of the biographical details about Christophe are taken from the opening chapter of this book.

3. Frère Christophe, 20.

4. Ibid., 84.

5. Ibid., 114.

6. Marie-Dominique Minassian, "Frère Christophe: Priant Parmi Les Priants," *Chemin de Dialogue* 27 (2006): 69–70.

7. Frère Christophe, 132.

8. Bruno Chenu, ed., *Sept vies pour Dieu et L'Élgérie* (Paris: Bayard Editions/Centurion, 1996), 149.

Chapter Ten: Witness to the Resurrection

1. Robert Masson, *Jusqu'au bout de La Nuit: L'Église D'Algérie* (Paris: cerf/Saint-Augustin, 1998), 188.

2. Pierre Claverie, OP, *La vie spirituelle,* 721 (1997): 767–68. This was a special issue of the magazine devoted to the memory of Pierre Claverie.

3. Jean-Jacques Pérennès, *Pierre Claverie: Un Algérien par alliance* (Paris: Les Editions du Cerf, 2000), 181. [This book has recently been translated into English: *A Life Poured Out: Pierre Claverie of Algeria,* Maryknoll, NY: Orbis Books, 2007.]

4. *La vie spirituelle,* 582.

5. Ibid., 724.

6. Ibid., 703.

7. Ibid., 748–752.

8. Pérennès, 390.

9. *La vie spirituelle,* 716.

10. Ibid., 716.

11. Ibid., 784.

12. Ibid., 770.

13. Ibid., 626.

14. Pérennès, 77–78.

Chapter Eleven: Encountering the Other

1. *Documentation Catholique* 1775 (1979): 1032–1044. The second document, referred to in a later chapter, is called *Les Églises du Maghreb en l'An 2000 (The Churches of the Maghreb in the Year 2000)*.

2. Ibid., 1034.

3. W. M. Abbot, SJ, ed., *The Documents of Vatican II, Gaudium et Spes*, para 22, (London-Dublin: Geoffrey Chapman, 1996), 222.

4. *Documentation Catholique* 1037.

5. Ibid., 1041.

6. Ibid., 1041.

7. Christoph Theobald, *Présences d'Évangile: Lire les Évangiles et l'Apocalypse en Algérie et ailleurs* (Paris: Les Editions de l'Atelier, 2003).

8. Ibid., 18.

9. Ibid., 18.

10. Abbot, *Lumen Gentium,* para 1, 15.

11. Theobald, 39.

12. Ibid., 43.

13. Ibid., 49.

14. Ibid., 113.

15. Armand Duval, *C'était une longue fidélité à l'Algérie et au Rwanda* (Paris: Médiaspaul, 1998), 88. A longer quotation from this letter is given in Chapter 6 on the White Fathers.

16. Henri Teissier, *Chrétiens En Algérie: Un Partage D'Espérance,* (Paris: Desclée De Brouwer, 2002).

17. Ibid., 77.

18. Ibid., 211.

Chapter Twelve: What Hope for the Future?

1. Henri Teissier, *Chrétiens en Algérie: Un Partage D'Espérance* (Paris: Desclée de Brouwer, 2002), 27.

2. Semaines Sociales de France, Session 2002, http://www.ssf-fr.org/archives/sessions/2002/textes/12_1.php3.

3. *Documentation Catholique* 2221 (2000): 230–241.

4. Ibid., 233.

5. Ibid., 237.

6. *La Semaine Religieuse d'Alger* 6 (2002): 143.

7. Henri Teissier, "Les axes de notre témoignage," Archives, Diocesan Office, 13, rue Khelifa Boukhalfa, Algiers.

8. Ibid., 4.

9. Eglise Evangélique Méthodiste: http://eemnews.umc-europe.org/2006/avril/11-12.php.

10. Claude Rault, "Billet Mensuel," Avril, 2006: http://amisdiocesesahara.free.fr/ltavr06.html.

11. *Actes de l'Assemblée Interdiocésaine,* Alger, 22–25 Septembre, 2004: Archives, Diocesan Office, 13, rue Khelifa Boukhalfa, Algiers.

12. Ibid., 89.

13. "Comme un mariage," *La Semaine Religieuse d'Alger* 6 (2005): 156.

14. Henri Teissier, 217.

Chapter Thirteen: God's Gift to Us

1. A biography of Msgr. Teissier has recently been published: Martine de Sauto, *Henri Teissier un évêque en Algerie* (Paris: Bayard, 2006).

2. André Barakat, "Temoignages lors du Jubilé," *La Semaine Religieuse d'Alger* 4 (2005): 91.

Appendix A: Reflection of Msgr. Teissier

Address Two: A Christian Church for a Muslim People

1. John Paul II, *Redemptoris Missio,* para 15 (London: Catholic Truth Society, 1991), 12.

2. International Theological Commission, "Le Christianisme et les religions" *Documentation Catholique* 2157 (1997): 312–332.

3. Agostino Trapé, *St. Augustin,* (Paris: Fayard, 1998), 287.

4. Vatican Council II, *Gaudium et Spes.*, para 1, p. 163, Austin Flannery, O.P., 1996, Costello Publishing Company, New York & Dominican Publications, Dublin.

Appendix B: Ribat es-Salam

1. Claude Rault, "Vers l'avenir," *Le Lien de La Paix,* 39, (2004): 1. (A special issue of the magazine of the Ribat group to celebrate its 25th anniversary)

2. Ibid., 2.

3. Ibid., 7–8.

4. Ibid., 7.

5. Ibid., 7–8.

6. In an email correspondence with the author in 2005.

7. Ibid., 9.

8. Ibid., 9.

9. Ibid., 21.

10. Ibid., 1.